The SURPRISE of
GERMANTOWN

To Bill Sharninghausen,
with best wishes,

Thomas J. McGuire

Cliveden, October 6, 1995

Frontispiece

An early 19th century view of the attack on Cliveden during the Battle of Germantown, October 4, 1777. Note the early 19th century uniforms on the American soldiers.

The S U R P R I S E *of*

GERMANTOWN,

or, The Battle of CLIVEDEN

October 4 $_{''}^{th}$ *1777*

by Thomas J. McGuire

Published by
CLIVEDEN of the National Trust
for Historic Preservation
and
Thomas Publications

To R.W.G.,
"Palmam qui meruit ferat."

Design and production:
    Bagnell & Socha

Cover:
    "Battle of Germantown," unknown artist,
    ca. 1790. Cliveden Collection.

Library of Congress Catalog Card Number: 94-68573
ISBN 0-939631-77-6

Printed in the United States of America
Published by THOMAS PUBLICATIONS
    353 Buford Avenue
    Gettysburg, PA 17325
    717.334.1921

Contents

I. Movements of the Armies
Prior to the Battle of Germantown 1

II. The British Occupation of Germantown 9

III. "We are always on the advance Post . . .
our Present One is unpleasant . . ." 21

IV. The 40th Regiment and Its Special Position 23

V. Washington Plans the Attack on Germantown...29

VI. The Night March to Germantown 33

VII. Phase I: The Battle Begins in Mount Airy 37

VIII. Phase II: Cliveden Becomes a
"Fortified Castle" 47

IX. Phase III: Musgrave's "Castle" under Attack 65

X. Mistaken Identity: The Collision
of Wayne and Stephen 79

XI. Retreat and Counterattack 82

XII. Aftermath of the Battle 85

XIII. Postscript 94

Glossary 95

Endnotes 96

Bibliography 116

List of Figures..119

Acknowledgments 120

Photo Credits 121

Colophon 122

List of Maps 122

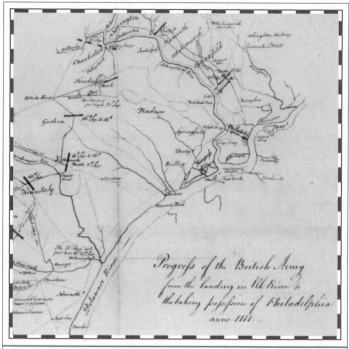

FIG. 1: *"Progress of the British Army from the Landing in Elk River to the Taking Possession of Philadelphia,"* John André, 1777

The map shows the "Surprise of Genl. Wayne 21$_{"}^{st}$ Sep:," also called the Paoli Massacre. The British camp at Valley Forge is also labelled "21$_{"}^{st}$ Sep:," and the British camp at Norriton between Swede's Ford and Stony Creek is shown just above the word "Plymouth," top right center. Germantown, or "German T.," appears north and slightly west of Philadelphia.

I.

Movements *of the* Armies Prior *to the* Battle *of* GERMANTOWN

Spring, 1777.

IN THE SPRING of 1777, the British decided on a strategy to split the American colonies by seizing control of the Hudson River Valley. The plan called for the convergence of three armies at Albany, New York. One force, under General Sir John Burgoyne, headed south from Quebec along Lake Champlain toward Albany. A second force, under General Barry St. Leger, was to leave Montreal and invade New York State from the west, moving through the Mohawk Valley. The third force, commanded by General Sir William Howe, the British Commander-in-Chief in North America, was to march northward from New York City and complete the linkup of the three armies at Albany.

Sir William Howe decided instead to capture Philadelphia, the capital of the Revolutionary government and the colonies' most important agricultural and commercial center. In his view, a successful Philadelphia campaign would cripple the rebellion and perhaps bring the war to an end.

The British force of 17,000 troops left New York Harbor on July 22, 1777.[1] Two hundred sixty-seven ships slowly proceeded down the New Jersey coast and by July 30 reached Delaware Bay. In a maneuver which baffled American forces, the flotilla shifted course on August 2 and headed south for the Chesapeake Bay.[2] Three weeks later, on August 25, the British army disembarked near Elkton, Maryland, some sixty miles south of Philadelphia.

For the next month, Howe's British, Hessian and Loyalist troops endured suffocating heat, drenching rain, uncertain roads and long marches through "strong," or hilly, country. Strictly forbidden to plunder, Howe's forces moved through a region inhabited by a largely neutral population.[3] At times, the roads and hills swarmed with parties of rebel dragoons (cavalry) and light infantry corps, resulting in a number of skirmishes. The British army encountered Washington's main Continental army at Brandywine Creek on September 11 and drove them from the field; Howe's army suffered serious casualties in the process. Exact numbers are difficult to ascertain, but the loss of 1000 men from Howe's army is not out of the question, despite the official British casualty report of 583.[4]

Washington's troops were in a more difficult position. Supplemented by state militias, the American

Commander-in-Chief had approximately 12,000 men at his disposal.[5] Supplies were uncertain, troop quality and discipline varied from unit to unit, and the seemingly endless marching and countermarching through the late summer took its toll on the men and equipment. The differences of opinion among the European professional officers, combined with the frustrations and jealousy expressed by many American-born officers over the promotion of "foreign experts," created tension and unnecessary disunity within the command structure.

Despite these problems, Washington's troops were generally in good spirits. At Brandywine, portions of the army fought extremely well. The loss that day was due more to faulty intelligence and overcaution than to a lack of resolve or bravery.

The two weeks that followed Brandywine were an infantryman's nightmare. During this period the Continentals crossed the Schuylkill River no fewer than three times and marched well over 100 miles, much of the time on mud-filled bottomless roads and without tents or baggage. The British infantry faced similar problems since their tents had been left on the ships in order to lighten the baggage train on the march.[6]

"The Paoli Massacre"
Sept.ʳ 20–21.ˢᵗ 1777.

At midday on September 16, the two armies met near Boot Tavern and Goshen Meeting House, but a heavy downpour prevented a major battle. Not long after, on the night of September 20–21, a British force commanded by Major General Charles Grey drove two Pennsylvania brigades, under the leadership of Brigadier General Anthony Wayne, from their position near the Paoli Tavern. Led by the 2nd Battalion of Light Infantry, the British swept through Wayne's camp just as the Pennsylvanians were departing. Part of Wayne's force moved in the wrong direction and was hit full-force by the British Light Infantry. The British cheered and charged with bayonets, killing between 50 and 100 Americans and wounding perhaps 150 others. They also took 71 prisoners, including 40 who were wounded.[7]

General Wayne had one stroke of luck that night when a British officer sent a squad to Wayne's home, "Waynesborough," only two miles from the encampment. Lieutenant Colonel Thomas Musgrave, commanding the

FIG. 2: "Battle of Paoli," Xavier Della Gatta, 1782

The attack on Wayne's camp near the Paoli Tavern at
1 A.M. on Sep.ͬ 21 left the Pennsylvania troops
thirsting for revenge.

British 40th and 55th regiments, moved toward the Paoli Tavern to block any American retreat in that direction. Musgrave sent a squad to Wayne's home, hoping that the Pennsylvania general might be spending the night with his family. The British searched the premises and departed emptyhanded, leaving the property undamaged.[8] Another, less civil British officer might have ordered the property destroyed.

The Pennsylvanians now had a score to settle. The fact that "The Affair of the Night of the 20th," also called "Wayne's Affair," and later, the "Paoli Massacre," was carried out in the middle of the night with bayonets fueled the Pennsylvanians' anger. To pour more salt in the wound, some of Wayne's subordinate commanders called his competence into question. One fact remained: the Pennsylvania regiments commanded by Generals Conway and Wayne were determined to repay the British Light Infantry for the attack on Paoli.[9]

For their part, the events of September 20 and 21 kept the British 2nd Battalion of Light Infantry on edge. Each man knew that the Pennsylvania

FIG. 3: Brig.$^{r}_{,,}$ Gen.$^{al}_{,,}$ Anthony Wayne (1745–96), James Sharples, S.$^{r}_{,,}$, 1796

His Pennsylvanians sought revenge for "Wayne's Affair" near Paoli. Their vengefulness was largely responsible for the stubborn British resolve to hold Cliveden at all costs.

FIG. 4: Detail, "Battle of Paoli"

*British officer bandaging his hand in left foreground is
Lieu.ᵗ Martin Hunter, Light Company, 52ᵈ Reg.ᵗ of Foot,
2ᵈ Battalion Light Infantry. The British officer lying dead
near him is Capt.ⁿ William Wolfe, Commander of the
40ᵗʰ Reg.ᵗ's Light Infantry Company.*

troops thirsted for revenge upon the "Bloodhounds," as
the Americans now termed the British Light Infantry.[10]
"Wayne's Affair" was, in fact, terrifying. The flash of bayonets and dragoon broadswords, the screams and cheers
in the night, the glow of the burning American "wigwams" and the bloody activities silhouetted in the dim
light formed, Lieutenant Martin Hunter wrote, " . . . alto-
gether one of the most dreadful scenes I ever beheld."[11]
Another officer, probably Lieutenant St. George, in writing to his fiancee, stated, "Then followed a dreadful
scene of havoc . . . The shrieks, groans, shouting, impre-
cations, deprecations . . . was more expressive of horror
than all the thunder of artillery, etc., on the day of
action."[12] Hunter and his friend, Lieutenant Mansart St.

George, were officers of the Light company of the 52nd Regiment of Foot, one of the thirteen companies in the 2nd Battalion of British Light Infantry. Both were young, adventuresome officers who received wounds during the campaign, St. George at the Battle of Brandywine, and Hunter at Paoli.[13] A Pennsylvania picket shot Hunter through the hand at close range, and though he continued to lead his men in the attack, he nearly fainted from the loss of blood. In the confusion of the night the battalion nearly left Hunter behind. Only Lieutenant St. George's insistence that the column halt until he was found saved Hunter from capture or death.[14]

On September 23, two days after Paoli, the British crossed the Schuylkill at Fatland Ford near Valley Forge and encamped in Norrington [Norristown] along Stony Run between the Schuylkill River at Swede's Ford and Germantown Road. Here they rested for a day before proceeding to Germantown on September 25.[15]

FIG. 5:
Johann Ewald: Captⁿ_" of Hessian Jagers [riflemen]

Ewald was stationed on Ridge Road near Wissahickon Creek. He later became a general in the Danish Army. He is here depicted in his Danish General's uniform.

II.
The British Occupation *of*
GERMANTOWN

❖ ❖ ❖ ❖ ❖ ❖ ❖ ❖ ❖ ❖ ❖ ❖ ❖

September 25ᵗʰ, 1777.

AT THE TIME OF THE REVOLUTION, a large number of German-speaking people lived above Philadelphia in an area to the north and east of the Schuylkill River. Many had emigrated from the Palatinate, a region along the Rhine River southwest of Frankfurt am Main. They belonged to a variety of religious groups, some of whom were pacifist. These people generally shared an ingrained fear of armies, especially the terrifying mercenary soldiers hired by German princes. Hessian mercenaries were among the most feared and despised of these troops.[16] Considering that a large portion of the King's army in Pennsylvania was comprised of Hessian soldiers, it is no surprise that the inhabitants greeted Howe's army with a combination of uncertainty, fear and anger. Captain Johann Ewald of the

Hessian Jager Corps commented in his journal about his entry into the region:

> This area is quite splendidly cultivated. The inhabitants are mostly Germans but were against us, the most ill-natured people in the world, who could hardly conceal their anger and hostile sentiments. One old lady, who was sitting on a bench before her front door, answered me in pure Palantine German when I rode up to her and asked her for a glass of water: 'Water I will give you, but I must also ask you: What harm have we people done to you, that you Germans come over here to suck us dry and drive us out of house and home? We have heard enough here of your murderous burning. Will you do the same here as in New York and the Jerseys? You shall get your pay yet!'[17]

The British army moved into Germantown in two columns. General Wilhelm von Knyphausen's column, headed by Captain Ewald and his jagers, marched along Ridge Road. The main column, commanded by Lord Cornwallis, moved over Germantown Road through Chestnut Hill and Mount Airy.[18] Sir William Howe and his staff accompanied this column. One of Howe's aides, Captain Friedrich von Munchhausen, a Hessian liaison officer, remarked in his journal:

> Lord Cornwallis' column . . . had an exceedingly pleasant march, because the road from

Chestnut Hill to Germantown is lined with many houses, most of them nice buildings. Along the way we found many inhabitants, mainly Germans, who spoke German among themselves.[19]

One of the non-German inhabitants of Germantown, twelve-year-old John Ashmead, remembered many years later the entry of the British Army into his home town:

> He [Ashmead] was allowed, unmolested, to set in the street porch. Their whole array seemed in complete order—the display of officers, the regular march of red-coated men, and refugee greens [American Loyalists], the highlanders [Scottish troops], grenadiers, their burnished arms, &c. There was, however, *no* display of colors [regimental flags] and *no* music—everything moved like machinery in silence.[20]

The march from the camp at Norrington was about twelve miles over dirt roads. The day was pleasant and the movement of close to 14,000 troops, including dragoons, artillery, and supply wagons, filled the air with dust.[21] Another observer of the army's march noticed that "The British

WEATHER REPORT:
Thursday, Sep.̸̸ 25
NEAR PHILADELPHIA

7 AM: 59 1/2° Bar. 30.00"
Wind: SE
Sunshine & Clouds

3 PM: 69° Bar. 29.875"
Wind: S
Cloudy

Began to rain in the afternoon & lasted all night. Cold rain.

—*Rev. Henry Muhlenberg, Trappe*

FIG. 6: Gen.ˡ̣ William Howe (1729–1814), 1780

Howe served as the British Commander-in-Chief in the American Colonies from 1776–78. His generally strong pro-American sympathies before the war may explain his relative disdain for battle during his period of service.

Army were covered with dust when they first passed through Germantown; they were at other times kept clean."[22]

The behavior of the Royal troops surprised many of the inhabitants. At first there was fear of looting or worse. Instead, the residents of Germantown found an army which initially exerted much effort to behave well. General Howe had issued strict orders at the beginning of the campaign which forbade plundering or destruction of private property owned by "well-disposed" inhabitants.[23] During the campaign, several soldiers were executed publicly for violation of these orders.[24] On the day that the British army entered Germantown, the orderly book of the 64th Regiment's Light Infantry Company noted:

Headquarters, September 25 . . . Pattroles to Be Sent frequently in order to keep the Soldiers out of the Village and Houses Adjacent . . . Major Maitland [commander of the 2nd Battalion Light Infantry] requests that officers will use their Utmost indeavour to prevent the men from doing Any harm to the inhabitants.[25]

Young John Ashmead recalled an incident when the British first entered Germantown:

In all their progress there was no violence or offence. Sundry men occasionally came up and said, 'Can you give us a little milk or any cider?' On being referred to the father, who purposely kept in door, as he was a known whig, it was deemed expedient to give out readily. In time, the cider barrel began to fall low, when it so occurred that a young officer came to ask a like indulgence; when it was said to him he was welcome, but others had been before him and left it muddy; he expressed his surprise at their exaction, and said it should be corrected. Quickly there appeared a sentinel before the house, who kept his place till superseded by another and another, for six or eight changes, until the whole army had passed. It showed discipline, and a decorous demeanor in an enemy, which it is but honest justice to record.[26]

FIG. 7: *"Battle of German Town,*
the 4ᵗʰ October 1777," John André, 1777

This map shows the British Army's position before
and during the battle. The dark parallel lines indicate
buildings along Germantown Road. Numerous fenced cross-
roads would hamper the troops, as did the many orchards
behind the houses, indicated by parallel blocks of dots. Note
that American troops are correctly positioned but identifica-
tion is confusing. The troops below Cliveden are marked
"Wayne and Sullivan," though "Sullivan and Wayne"
would place them properly on the map. "Sterling and Nash"
should read "Greene and Stephen"; Stirling and Nash
were in reserve, near Chew's house.

DETAIL 7a: *The camp of the 2ᵈ Battⁿ of Light Infantry appears in the left center of the map and is labelled "First Attack of the Rebels at day break on the 2d Lt. Inf:"; note light infantry position on both sides of Germantown Road.*

DETAIL 7b: *André notes "Chew's House" with the inscription "Col. Musgrave took post with part of the 40th Regimt. in Mr. Chews House covering the retreat of the Light Inf and maintaining himself for above an hour against several pcs of Arty. and a very considerable force." Note 40ᵗʰ Regiment's position to the right, or BEHIND, the house.*

DETAIL 7c: *To the right center is Luken's mill, misnamed "Lewis's Mill" and the inscription " a Flanker of the Rebels was taken by a Centry from this post who gave the first information of the intended attack."*

The main British camp followed a line parallel to School House Lane, from the mouth of the Wissahickon Creek through the center of Germantown near Market Square. It continued toward Frankford Creek, with outposts as far east as Kensington. Advance posts watched the main roads leading to the camp from the north. Hessian jagers, commanded by Colonel von Wurmb, occupied an outpost on Ridge Road, north of Wissahickon Creek near the country seat of Dr. William Smith, provost of the College of Philadelphia [University of Pennsylvania]. The 2nd Battalion of British Light Infantry, commanded by Major Maitland, was based at

*FIG. 8: William Allen
(1704–1780)
by* Robert Feke, 1746

William Allen was a merchant, lawyer and judge whose country house Mount Airy sat atop the hill where British pickets fired the first shots of the battle. Allen's sons William, Jr. and Andrew accompanied the British Army on their march into Germantown on September 25, 1777.

Mount Pleasant, a small hill located on Germantown Road two miles north of Market Square. Pickets for this unit were posted at Mount Airy, the country seat of William Allen, some 400 yards north of the light infantry camp. Major Abercromby positioned his First Battalion of British Light Infantry at Luken's Mill, with advance posts near the crossroads of Lime-kiln Pike and Abington Road [Washington Lane]. In case of a major attack, both outposts could be supported by the British 40th Regiment of Foot, commanded by Lieutenant Colonel Musgrave, stationed behind Chief Justice Benjamin Chew's country seat, Cliveden. The American Loyalist unit, known as the Queen's Rangers or Wemyss's Corps for its commander, Captain James Wemyss, covered the far right flank.[27]

Light Troops.

Light infantry companies from various regiments were brought together to form the two battalions of British Light Infantry in Germantown. After the French and Indian War, British regiments added light infantry companies to protect the advance and flanks of the army while marching or in battle. The light infantry companies also formed encampment outposts when the army was on campaign.

The composition of the light infantry battalions varied. In the Philadelphia campaign, men from the light companies of thirteen different regiments, including the 40th, 52nd and the 64th, formed the Second Battalion of British Light Infantry. Similarly, the grenadier companies

FIG. 9: Cliveden, Country Seat of Benjamin Chew,
Built 1763–68 and Site of the Primary Action
of the Battle of Germantown

This undated view shows Cliveden on the right, Germantown
Avenue, and on the left, the Papen-Johnson House, built in
1698 and demolished in the late 19th century.

of the British army were also placed together into battalions. The grenadier and light infantry companies formed the "flank" companies, and were considered the elite soldiers in the regiment.[28]

PHILADELPHIA
26ᵗʰ of September 1777.

On the morning of September 26, Lord Cornwallis marched the British and Hessian grenadier battalions, along with several artillery pieces, to take possession of Philadelphia itself. These smartly dressed troops, the cream of the army, tied greenery to their caps and to the artillery horses, adding a festive air to their entrance. The troops involved in this initial occupation force numbered about 3000.[29]

British engineers immediately constructed artillery batteries both north and south of the city to prevent attacks by the Pennsylvania Navy which still controlled the Delaware River. The next day, September 27, the

---

WEATHER REPORT:
Friday, 26 Sepᵣ
NEAR PHILADELPHIA

7 AM: 51° Bar. 30.175"
Wind: NW
Sunshine

3 PM: 64° Bar. 30.2"
Wind: NW
Sunshine

WEATHER REPORT:
Saturday, 27 Sep$_n^r$
NEAR PHILADELPHIA

7 AM: 47° Bar. 30.35"
Wind: NE
Fair

3 PM: 61° Bar. 30.325"
Wind: NE
Sunshine & Clouds

Royal Engineers made preliminary surveys for the construction of a line of earthen forts called *redoubts* north of the city beginning just below Kensington on the Delaware and running west to the hill called Fairmount on the Schuylkill River.[30] While these defenses rose, the main British force would remain at Germantown.

Shelter for the troops was of paramount concern to the British commanders. The army tents had been left on the ships to lighten the baggage train on the march, so the soldiers received instructions to build huts or "wigwams," as the British termed them. The company order for the 2nd Battalion of British

FIG. 10: Lord Cornwallis (1738–1805), 1786

Cornwallis and troops entered Philadelphia in triumph on September 26 while their band played "God Save the King."

Light Infantry stated on September 27, "The Companys to make Wigwams as fast as possible, the QMr. [Quartermaster] Will attend & show thier Ground."[31] Following those orders the soldiers assembled fence rails, set at a 45° angle, around a center pole and covered the outside with straw, sod, corn stalks and tree boughs.[32] The plans called for the British troops to remain camped in their wigwams until the tents could be brought up from the fleet.

FIG. 11:
Wigwams from Della Gatta *Painting, "Battle of Paoli"*

Wigwams, sometimes spelled "wigwarms,"
were temporary huts made of fence rails, tree boughs,
cornstalks, hay, sod and other such materials. Both armies
made extensive use of wigwams to avoid using tents which
would burden their march with long baggage trains.
An officer of the 1st Battalion British light infantry noted:

"Position taken up during rain [Sept. 25] and not on
ground originally intended; Army by mistake not halted
soon enough;—men having made themselves comfortable,
out of consideration camp of wigwams not altered."

III.

"We *are* ALWAYS *on the advance* Post . . . *our* Present One *is* UNPLEASANT . . ."

THE MEN AND OFFICERS of the 2nd Battalion of British Light Infantry were on edge. As a matter of fact, they were on *the* edge, the cutting edge of the British army. These troops were constantly "on the point;" performing the risky tasks of forming the vanguard and rear guard on the march, patrolling the flanks and occupying the forward posts of the camp. The soldiers were tough; the best of them were small, wiry, agile men unafraid of the rigors of dangerous and dirty work. Private John Waites was typical of the light infantrymen. A member of the Light Company of the 52nd Regiment of Foot, John Waites stood about 5 feet 6 inches tall and was in his mid 30s. Later accounts described him as "having lived a rugged existence."[33]

After Paoli, members of the 2nd Battalion of British Light Infantry were apprehensive. Lieutenant Martin

Hunter wrote, "I don't think that our battalion slept very soundly after that night for a long time."[34] For the last few nights in September 1777, American patrols alarmed the Light Infantry outposts near Germantown. Lieutenant St. George wrote, "They threaten retaliation, vow they will give no quarter . . . We are always on the advance post of the army; our present one is unpleasant . . . There has been firing this night all around our sentries . . ."[35] The constant tension took its toll on nerves. Nonetheless, accustomed to difficult tasks, the British Light Infantry remained alert for trouble.

FIG. 12: Maj.ʳ John André (1751–1780), Adjutant Genᵃˡ of the British Forces in America

André, wearing the uniform of a British officer, drew the most accurate maps of the Philadelphia campaign, including the Battle of Germantown (see Figures 1 and 7). André was a talented and charming man, respected by the British and Americans alike. He is most famous for conspiring with the traitorous American General Benedict Arnold. André was caught with Arnold's secret descriptions of the American fortification at West Point. With principle outweighing personal affection, Washington had André hanged. Arnold escaped to the British lines, and by prearrangement assumed the rank of General and served in the British Army until the conclusion of the war. As might be expected, the British distrusted him nearly as much as the Americans.

IV.

The 40th Regiment *and* Its
S P E C I A L   P O S I T I O N

LIEUTENANT COLONEL THOMAS MUSGRAVE surveyed his assigned position in Germantown with satisfaction. His regiment, the British 40th Regiment of Foot, was stationed halfway between the main British camp along School House Lane and the dangerous out-posts occupied by the 1st and 2nd Battalions of British Light Infantry. The 1st Battalion was posted about one mile east of the 40th's camp, near the crossroads of Limekiln Pike and Abington Road, while the 2nd Battalion occupied Mount Pleasant, about one mile north on Germantown Avenue from Musgrave's position. Musgrave's location behind Cliveden placed him ideally to support the light infantry battalions should the rebel army attack the British forces.[36]

Colonel Musgrave was no stranger to the rigors of war and the difficult task of the light infantry. During the

FIG. 13: Lieut.ʼ Col.ʼ Thomas Musgrave (1737–1812),
Engraving Done *in* 1797 *from a* Portrait Painted 1786

Musgrave commanded the 40.ᵗʰ Reg.ʼ of Foot which occupied
Cliveden during the Battle of Germantown. While Musgrave
went on to an illustrious career in the British army he always
considered the Battle of Germantown as his greatest triumph.
This engraving, and the portrait upon which it is based, shows
Cliveden to his right. Another portrait of the same period
shows Musgrave holding a plan for the battle.

New York campaign the previous year, he commanded the light company of the 64th Regiment of Foot and won regard as an expert in the field of "partisan" or "ranger" tactics, as the light infantry maneuvers were termed. The day before the Battle of White Plains, Thomas Musgrave was shot in the face, leaving him permanently disfigured.[37] The artist who painted his portrait a decade later was kind, as the picture gives the viewer no clue that Musgrave had a hole in his left cheek. The portrait shows Musgrave posing against a fence, with the 40th Regiment's camp and his famous post, Cliveden, over his left shoulder.[38]

The 40th Regiment had already seen hard service in America.[39] Musgrave took the place of Lieutenant Colonel Grant, who was killed in action at the Battle of Long Island. The regiment was seriously weakened, largely due to its involvement in the Battle of Princeton in early 1777.[40] As of March 1778, the Americans still held eighty-five of its soldiers, including noncommissioned officers and one drummer.[41] The official regimental strength list for units embarking from New York for the Philadelphia campaign records that the 40th Regiment had eight companies totalling 320 men, or an average of forty men per company.[42] The remaining two "flank companies," the grenadier and light infantry companies, were removed from the unit and battalioned together with the flank companies of other regiments.

The Light Infantry Company of the 40th Regiment, initially commanded by Captain William Wolfe, joined twelve other light companies to form the 2nd Battalion of British Light Infantry, commanded by Major Maitland. Captain Wolfe was killed at the Paoli Massacre, the only

British officer to fall that night. Captain William Montgomery, who commanded one of the 40th's battalion companies, replaced Wolfe on September 21. Captain William Harris in turn took Montgomery's former position.[43]

The Grenadier Company of the 40th Regiment, commanded by Captain John Graves Simcoe, was on occupation duty in Philadelphia after September 26 along with the other grenadier companies. On October 15, after the Battle of Germantown, Simcoe was transferred to command the most famous Loyalist unit of the Revolution, the Queen's Rangers.[44] Captain James Wemyss, another officer of the 40th Regiment of Foot, was Simcoe's predecessor. This battalion of green-clad Loyal Americans, also known as "Tories," "refugees" or "cowboys" is frequently referred to during the Philadelphia Campaign as "Wemyss's Corps."

Wemyss, Simcoe and Musgrave were recognized experts in the field of light infantry tactics. It is no surprise that Sir William Howe, himself a light infantry expert, positioned the 40th Regiment in a strategic location so as to support the light infantry outposts in case of attack. At least two respected American officers later believed that Colonel Musgrave had planned to use Benjamin Chew's country house Cliveden as a fortress long before an attack took place. "If he did," wrote Major John Eager Howard of the 4th Maryland Regiment, "he certainly shewed his military judgment."[45]

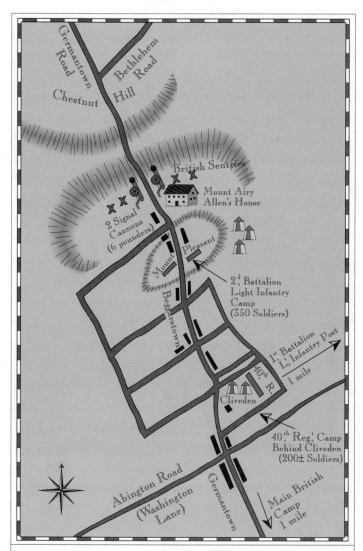

MAP 1. *The Position of British Outposts near Cliveden*

Fig. 14: Gen! George Washington (1732–1799)
by James Peale, 1787–90

Washington's complex plan for Germantown required
that his army split into four main divisions to spring a trap
on the British in Philadelphia. The vagaries of weather, which
reduced visibility and communication, combined with the
British occupation of Cliveden proved
disastrous to the Americans.

V.

WASHINGTON
Plans *the* Attack
on GERMANTOWN

October, 1777.

IN RETROSPECT, the military career of George Washington is somewhat puzzling. On the one hand, he arrived at daring battle schemes, such as that planned for attacking the British camp at Germantown; yet he showed indecisiveness that resulted in losses like Brandywine. It is also difficult to reconcile his actions while the British were planning to cross the Schuylkill River on September 22 and 23. In response to a British reconnaissance patrol near French Creek and a small but noisy force of Hessians crossing the Schuylkill at Gordon's Ford [Phoenixville], Washington pulled his army away from the river fords and fell back to Faulkner's Great Swamp near Pottsgrove and Limerick.

While the American supply base at Reading had to be protected, this drastic maneuver allowed the British army to cross the Schuylkill unhindered and take Philadelphia at leisure. It is possible that the scene was too similar to Brandywine; numerous fording places might allow his army to be outflanked again. The attack on Wayne's camp two nights before might also have made the American Commander-in-Chief more cautious. Whatever the reason, Washington's critics had plenty of grist for their mills regarding the failure of the Continental Army to adequately protect Philadelphia.

After the British entered Germantown on September 25 and occupied Philadelphia on the 26th, Washington called a council of war to ask his general officers their opinions about the feasibility of an attack. They agreed on a "wait-and-see" approach, knowing all too well that a full-scale attack on the British army could injure the Continental Army beyond repair.[46]

The situation soon changed. Washington moved his army from Faulkner's Great Swamp near Limerick to Methacton Hills in Worcester Township. There on October 2, he received information from a captured British courier that a large British force had left Germantown for Chester on September 30. This detachment, comprised of the British 10th Regiment of Foot and the 42nd, or Royal Highland Regiment, less-

---

WEATHER REPORT:
Thursday, Oct.ʳ, 2
NEAR PHILADELPHIA

7 AM: 52° Bar. 30.35"
Wind: NW
Fair

3 PM: 64° Bar. 30.3"
Wind: WSW
Fair

"Weather vastly fine. Foggy mornings."

—Montresor

ened Howe's force at Germantown by 1000 men.[47] In addition, there were 3000 British and Hessian troops in Philadelphia with another 2000 in Wilmington. There also were casualties, the sick and those "on duty." This left 7000 to 8000 men as the effective British force in Germantown.[48] Washington recognized that General Howe had divided his force and that this represented the best chance for a successful attack. If the Americans waited much longer, the British would complete their fortifications north of Philadelphia, making a frontal attack suicidal.

Washington's plan called for four columns to hit the British camp at Germantown. Two center columns, made up of regular Continental troops, were to converge on the center of the main British camp after overwhelming the outposts. The right and left wings of the attack, comprised of militia regiments from Pennsylvania, New Jersey and Maryland, were to attack the left and right flanks of Howe's army. A small "fifth column," strictly a diversion, was to be sent down the west side of the Schuylkill River to draw the attention of the British pickets at Middle Ferry [Market Street Bridge]. The latter scheme was intended to divert the British grenadiers in Philadelphia and prevent them from reinforcing the army in Germantown.[49] If all went according to plan, the British would be dislodged from their position and compelled to evacuate Philadelphia. The political repercussions of such an event could be quite significant for the British government.

Washington's strategy for Germantown was one of his most daring and intricate plans attempted during the Revolution. It involved moving some 12,000 men divided into four columns a distance of between fourteen and twenty miles, depending on the column's assigned attack position. It required both silence on the march over dark roads and determination in the attack. Above all, it had to be coordinated. Military experts later commented that the plan's major flaw was its complexity and overambitiousness; the audacity of the endeavor impressed friend and foe alike.[50]

FIG. 15: Maj.ʳ Gen.ˡ John Sullivan (1740–1795), 1776

This romantic and imaginary engraved portrait of Sullivan was executed in England to satisfy English curiosity about the appearance of significant American soldiers. Besides his war service, Sullivan was a member of the First and Second Continental Congresses and the New Hampshire Constitutional Convention.

VI.

The Night March *to*
GERMANTOWN

✤ ✤ ✤ ✤ ✤ ✤ ✤ ✤ ✤ ✤ ✤ ✤ ✤ ✤

6:00 P.M., Octb'r. yᵉ third, 1777.

THE ORDER OF BATTLE appeared fairly straight-
forward, yet the execution of the march resulted in
delay and confusion. The movement of thousands of
men in four columns, plus artillery and ammunition wagons, seemed to take forever. Some troops began the
march at 6:00 p.m., October 3; all the men were on the
march by 9:00 p.m. The extreme right flank of
Washington's force, General Armstrong's Pennsylvania
Militia, was to march south on the "Ridge or
Manatawney Road" [Ridge Pike], to attack the Hessians
at the mouth of the Wissahickon Creek. General Thomas
Conway's brigade led the right-center of the American
army, followed by General John Sullivan's Maryland
troops and General Anthony Wayne's Pennsylvanians.

They were to march "above Manatawny Road," which meant that they should have been on Germantown Road, but they actually moved south on Skippack Road to Bethlehem Pike. Upon arrival in Germantown they were to attack the outpost of the 2nd Battalion of British Light Infantry at William Allen's house, Mount Airy.

Major General Nathanael Greene's division, the bulk of the attacking force, made up the left-center of the American line. Originally assigned to travel over Skippack Road, these men instead moved over Morris Road, which delayed their march. The extreme left flank, made up of Smallwood's Maryland militia and Forman's New Jersey militia, was to head down Morris Road to Church Road, advancing ahead of Greene's column. From St. Thomas's Church, Whitemarsh, they were to march to Old York Road and turn right toward the center of Germantown. Greene's column was to turn down Limekiln Pike and attack the 1st Battalion of British Light Infantry posted near Luken's Mill.[51]

Despite the optimism of the orders of battle, which asserted that all troops were to be in position by 2:00 a.m., rest until 4:00 a.m. and begin a coordinated attack at 5:00 a.m., none of the columns arrived on schedule. The march lasted all night. Officers

---

WEATHER REPORT:
Friday, Oct.ʳ 3
NEAR PHILADELPHIA

7 AM: 51° Bar. 30.35"
Wind: SW
Fair

3 PM: 69° Bar. 30.3"
Wind: SW
Sunshine & Clouds

"The mornings very foggy, but the weather fine."—Montresor

"The night was dark and it looked like rain, but it remained dry.".
—Rev. Henry Muhlenberg, Trappe

permitted no lights and enforced strict silence. The night was cloudy and the air damp and chilly. Men received pieces of white paper to place in their hats so that they could see each other in the dark.[52]

Perhaps it was a lucky accident that the march took as long as it did, for the British received several warnings of an impending attack and sent out patrols. The last entry made in Captain Thomas Armstrong's orderly book for the 64th Regiment of Foot Light Infantry Company states, "After orders 8 at night 3d. Octor. 1777—The 55th, 57th, 63d., 64th, 71st, 37th & 40th companys to parade with arms & accoutrements at Major Maitland's Quarters immedi-

FIG. 16: Maj.ʳ Gen.ˡ Nathanael Greene (1742–86) by Charles Willson Peale, 1784

The late arrival of Greene's division caused confusion in the American ranks: Woodford's Brigade assaulted the rear of Cliveden while Stephen's men fired into Wayne's troops by mistake.

ately."[53] This patrol, made up of half of the light infantry companies of the 2nd Battalion of British Light Infantry, went out on patrol as far as Whitemarsh where they discovered some fires burning.[54] They must have missed the American columns advancing in that area by only a few minutes.

About 2:00 a.m., a picket from the 1st Battalion of British Light Infantry posted at Limekiln Pike and Abington Road captured "a rebel flanker who claimed he was a deserter."[55] When taken to Major Abercromby, the commander of the 1st Battalion of British Light Infantry, the deserter disclosed the planned attack. Abercromby sent the man to the main headquarters where he was put into the guardhouse because the officer on duty, Major Nesbit Balfour, was "too lazy to get up and examine him."[56] Abercromby informed Generals James Grant and William Erskine of the man's story; these officers gave orders to "alert and accoutre." Grant and Erskine later rode to headquarters and found the man in the guardhouse, unexamined.[57] Thus, there was a delay in alerting the entire army of the impending attack. Almost unbelievably, "The 2nd L[ight] I[nfantry] & 40th Regt. Encamp'd at the Head of Germantown & a mile in Front of the Line were *by mistake missed in the Order to Accoutre.*"[58]

Manner of the Capture of Prisoner

"On the Lime Kiln road one sentry was posted; two was usually posted on high road. This being a cross road, and near other sentries one had been judged sufficient.—Sentry heard a man approaching; bent on one knee, thought him armed and a deserter, but resolved to secure him; night dark; man approached close; sentry challenged gently; answer it is I; it is Trynn, don't you know me; Throw down your arms or I will put you to death. Prisoner surprised surrendered. told him he had been on the flanking party; stopped for a particular occasion; afterwards went on but not meeting the party; had got on the road and continued his march thinking the party forward.—"

Unidentified Capt$_n^n$, 1$_n^{st}$ Batt$_n^n$ British L.I.

Unpublished manuscript, private collec$_n^n$

VII.
Phase I: *The* Battle Begins *in*
MOUNT AIRY

5:30 A.M., 4ᵗʰ October 1777.

THE OFFICERS of Captain Jacob Bower's Company of the Sixth Pennsylvania Regiment of the Continental Line under the field command of Lieutenant Colonel Josiah Harmar, the lead regiment in Brigadier General Thomas Conway's Brigade, were in familiar territory. Lieutenant John Markland was born in Philadelphia in 1755, as was Lieutenant James Glentworth. Ensign Charles Mackinett, also twenty-two years old, was a native of Germantown. His widowed mother kept the "Green Tree Tavern, known also as Widow Mackinett's Tavern," just down Germantown Road from Colonel Musgrave's 40th Regiment encampment behind Cliveden.[59] The war was at the very doorsteps of these men.

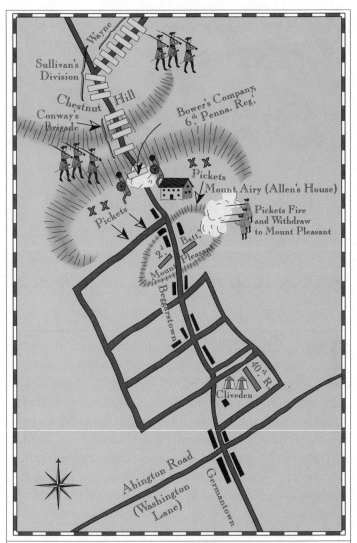

MAP 2. *Opening Positions 5:30 A.M. yᵉ 4ᵗʰ Octʳ*

Bower's Company of the 6ᵗʰ Pₐ. Regᵗ attacks the Light Infantry outpost at Allen's House; Pickets fire both signal guns and withdraw to Mount Pleasant.

The Sixth Pennsylvania Regiment was the first American infantry unit in action on the morning of October 4. Sometime between 5:00 a.m. and 5:30 a.m. [there was no "standard time" and the accounts vary], this regiment moved silently in column at the head of Conway's brigade down the south slope of Chestnut Hill along Germantown Road. Marching with fixed bayonets, they advanced up the rise of Mount Airy along with a troop of dragoons. Their orders were to silence the British pickets with bayonets and sabers to prevent the alarm from being sounded.[60]

Suddenly the dark quiet of the early morning was punctuated by gunfire. Musket shots from the British pickets at Mount Airy alerted the Light Infantry camp on Mount Pleasant, 400 yards to the rear. The American scheme to silence the sentries failed. The pickets fired as quickly as they could at the column approaching up Germantown Road.

An ear-shattering blast, quickly followed by another, shook the Pennsylvanians as the British fired the two light six-pounder alarm cannons. The artillerymen reloaded rapidly and managed to loose several more rounds before they and the sentries retired from Mount Airy. They fell back to the safety of the camp of the 2nd Battalion of British Light Infantry, shouting the alarm.

The sound travelled for quite a distance. It alerted the main British camp, located two miles south of the 2nd Battalion's outpost, and General Howe's Hessian aide, Captain Friedrich von Munchhausen, reported hearing guns at half past five while delivering a message to Lord Cornwallis near Philadelphia. He gave the message to His Lordship and also informed him of the signal guns, after which von Munchhausen rode as quickly as possible back toward the scene of the action, some seven or eight miles away.[61]

Atmospheric Conditions

Dawn broke just as the pickets were attacked. The sun came out for several minutes but was soon covered again by clouds.[62] The damp, cool ground combined with the warmer air to create a ground fog that became impenetrable in some places, unnoticeable in other places. These conditions caused the thick white gunpowder smoke to hang in the air, reducing visibility to near zero. Field stubble ignited by the muzzle flashes of cannon and muskets smoldered, adding to the acrid battle smog. The confusion of the subsequent battle and some of the odd occurrences of the day resulted directly from a lack of visibility.

WEATHER REPORT:
Saturday, Oct.ʳ 4
NEAR PHILADELPHIA

7 AM: 58° Bar. 30.35"
Sunshine & Clouds

3 PM: 71° Bar. 30.275"
Wind: SW
Sunshine & Clouds

A fog early this morning.

The Battle at Mount Pleasant

When the two alarm guns fired, the camp of the 2nd Battalion of British Light Infantry was instantly under arms. Some of the men ran out the back part of their huts, having the memory of the Paoli Massacre in their minds and being fearful that the Americans were already in their camp. The available force, numbering about 350, fixed bayonets and braced themselves for the attack.[63]

Captain Bower's Company of the 6th Pennsylvania, with Lieutenants Markland and Glentworth along with Ensign Mackinett, advanced towards the Light Infantry. Lieutenant Martin Hunter of the British 52nd Regiment heard the Pennsylvanians shout, "Have at [i.e. "fire at"] the bloodhounds! Avenge Wayne's affair!," accompanied by a volley.[64] Hunter saw his friend Lieutenant St. George fall, shot in the head. Private Peacock of the 52nd picked the fallen officer up and carried him to the rear. The British returned fire, both with muskets and cannon[65] (see Fig. 26a on page 63).

A six-pound ball screamed through the air near Lieutenant Markland, striking Private Abraham Best and tearing off one of his legs below the knee. Best's blood covered Markland's pantaloons. The private was placed in an ammunition wagon appropriated for the wounded and sent to an army hospital at Reading.[66]

The British Light Infantry let out a cheer and charged Conway's men. The left of Conway's brigade gave way. Bower's company was ordered to move up and support the left of the line; after heavy fighting they forced the Light Infantry to fall back. A seesaw action developed as the British reformed and charged again. Once more, part of Conway's line gave way, only to reform and once more renew the attack.[67]

FIG. 17:
*John Eager Howard
(1752–1827), 1782
by* Charles Willson Peale

The 4ᵗʰ Maryland Regᵗ led by Majʳ John Eager Howard passed Cliveden early in the battle. Later, his unit fired at the 40ᵗʰ Regᵗ as Musgrave's men came out of Cliveden to pursue the retreating Continentals; Howard's muskets "checked" the 40ᵗʰ's pursuit. Howard's valor at the Battle of Cowpens in 1781 earned him a Congressional medal, seen here in his lapel button He married Peggy Chew, daughter of Benjamin Chew of Cliveden, in 1787.

Behind Conway's Brigade, the rest of this American column prepared for battle. Sullivan's Maryland troops formed west of Germantown Avenue on Allen's Lane. Their left flank rested two hundred yards from William Allen's house, Mount Airy.[68] Wayne's Brigade formed up on the east side of Germantown Road. Both forces moved to support Conway's men who were mostly on the road itself and in the fields immediately on either side.

When these American forces arrived, the British Light Infantry found themselves completely outflanked and hopelessly outnumbered. The Light Infantry camp was on both sides of Germantown Road and the British position was untenable. Wayne's troops attacked the British with a vengeance. Remem-

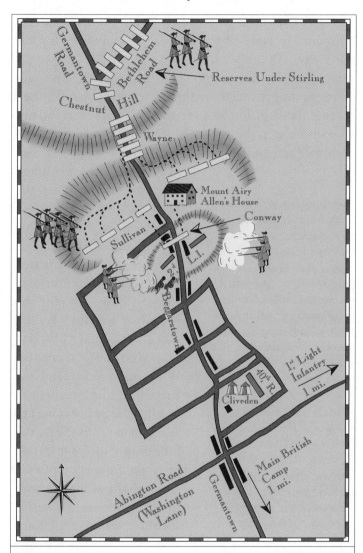

MAP 3. The Fight at Mount Pleasant
5:45 A.M.–6:15 A.M.

bering the night of September 20 they refused to take prisoners. In spite of the officers' attempts to stop the butchery, Wayne's brigade bayonetted every Light Infantryman who fell into their hands.[69] With the suddenness and ferocity of this new attack by Wayne's Brigade the British troops began to fall back. For the first time in the war, the trumpeter of the Light Infantry had to sound "retreat." At first, it was difficult to get the men to fall back. Then, the British line melted away as the Light Infantry broke.

General Sir William Howe, the British Commander-in-Chief, hurried with his staff up Germantown Road toward the sound of battle.[70] Somewhere between Cliveden and Mount Pleasant, Sir William encountered the British Light Infantry in headlong retreat. Howe had been instrumental in the founding and organization of Light Infantry and considered them his favorite troops.[71] He was shocked to see these proud, disciplined soldiers in full flight before the Americans. Howe's aide, Captain von Munchhausen, who had delivered the message to Cornwallis

". . . On the first shots being fired at our picquet the battalion was out and under arms in a minute; so much had they in recollection Wayne's affair [the Paoli massacre] that many of them rushed out at the back of their huts. At this time the day had broke about five minutes, but it was a very thick, foggy morning, and so dark that we could not see a hundred yards before us. Just as the battalion had formed the picquet ran in and said the enemy were advancing in force." They had not well joined the battalion when we heard a loud cry of 'Have at the Bloodhounds! Avenge Wayne's affair!' and immediately fired a volley. We gave them another in return, cheered, and charged. As it was the close of the campaign, our battalion was very weak. They did not consist of more than three hundred and fifty men, and there was no support nearer than Germantown, a mile in our rear . . . We charged them twice, till the battalion was so reduced by killed and wounded that the bugle was sounded to retreat . . . they all retreated to Germantown . . ."

—Journal of Lt Martin Hunter

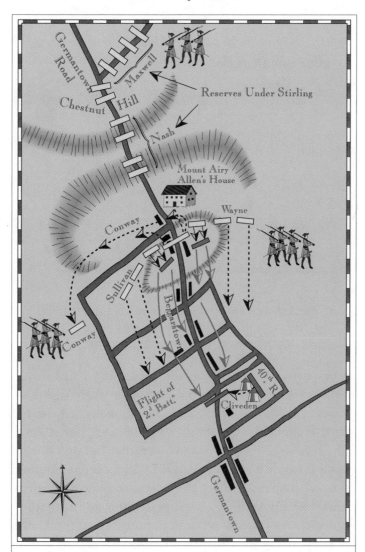

MAP 4. *The British Flee from* MOUNT PLEASANT
6:15 A.M.–6:30 A.M.

FIG. 18:
*"Gin, Engine for drawing the Fuzes out of the Shell,
Box with grapeshot, Section of a Petard," 1779*

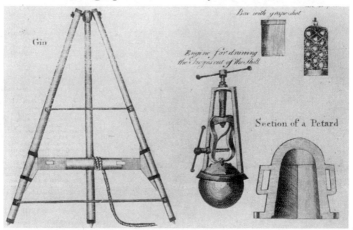

*Grapeshot, an anti-personnel projectile, scatters small
iron balls in a deadly hail. When fired from a cannon,
the effect is similar to a shotgun blast.*

earlier, arrived in time "to see something I had never seen before, namely the English in full flight."[72] Lieutenant Martin Hunter of the 52nd Light Infantry heard General Howe shout, "For shame! For shame, light infantry! I never saw you retreat before! Form! Form! It's only a scouting party!"[73] A round of grapeshot from an American artillery piece slammed into a tree near Howe and his staff. Lieutenant Hunter and the other light infantry officers were delighted to see the Commander-in-Chief and his entourage scatter as the grapeshot rattled about their ears. The appearance of Sullivan's and Wayne's forces further made clear that Howe's chastisement was undeserved.[74]

VIII.
Phase II: Cliveden *Becomes a* "FORTIFIED CASTLE"

LIEUTENANT COLONEL Thomas Musgrave quickly formed the British 40th Regiment's battalion companies after the alarm guns sounded. The firing north of his encampment grew more intense and moved closer toward his position as the battle developed. General Howe and his staff rode up Germantown Avenue past Cliveden to view the situation firsthand. As Howe recognized that the Americans were launching a full-scale attack, he ordered Musgrave's 40th Regiment to support the light infantry and cover their retreat.[75]

The British situation changed by the minute. The 2nd Battalion of Light Infantry put up a fight at every fence, ditch and hedge. The American advance was fluid. The Continentals near the road slowly moved forward against opposition, while the right of Sullivan's line and the left of Wayne's brigade encountered little or no oppo-

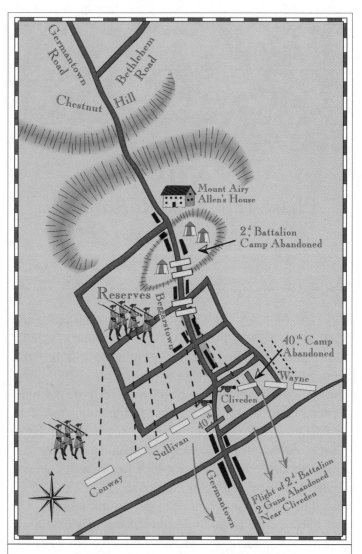

MAP 5. *The 40.ᵗʰ Covers the Retreat of the*
2.ᵈ Batt.ⁿ of Light Infantry and
Occupies Cliveden 6:15 A.M.

sition. Thus, the light infantry found themselves constantly outflanked by the sheer size of the American line. Retreat was the only reasonable course of action since Wayne's men were "giving no quarter," that is, taking no prisoners. Colonel Musgrave ordered the 40th Regiment to help cover the light infantry's withdrawal. By

FIG. 19: Facsimile of William Harris's Signature

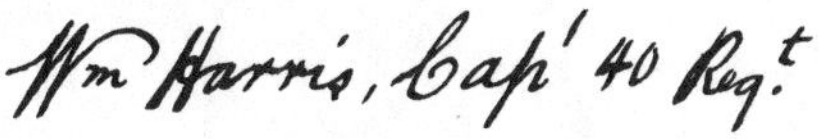

the time the battle reached the vicinity of Cliveden the retreat had become a rout. The light infantry abandoned their two six-pounder artillery pieces on Germantown Road near Cliveden. The Royal artillerymen also slashed the dragropes and killed their horses to prevent the Continentals from putting them to immediate use.[76]

Part of the 40th had moved to cover the retreat when Musgrave was informed that some American troops were already in the 40th's camp behind Cliveden. These were men from the extreme left flank of Wayne's brigade. Wayne's men advanced quickly and eagerly into the fray despite having to dismantle numerous fences which made proper battle alignment difficult.[77] The Pennsylvanians effectively threatened Musgrave's line of retreat.[78] Realizing the danger of this situation, Musgrave ordered part of the 40th Regiment to stay with the light infantry, while the rest of the regiment, numbering between 100 and 120 men, went into Cliveden.[79]

Colonel Musgrave directed the heavy window shutters on the ground floor to be secured and the doors barricaded. Captain William Harris, whose name has been

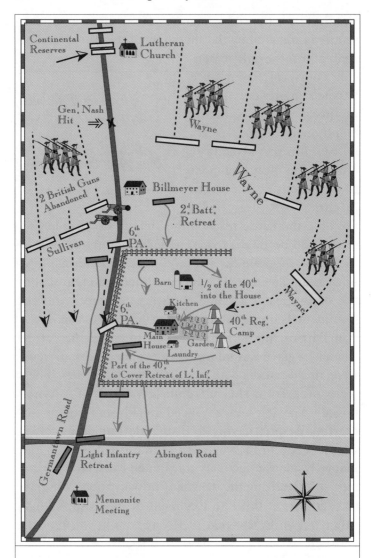

MAP 6. *1ˢᵗ Maneuvers around Cliveden*
6:30 A.M.–6:45 A.M.

FIG. 20a: American Rifleman
& Penns.$_{,,}^{ia}$ Infantryman,
German Engraving, 1784

The American Rifleman, dress'd in a long
fring'd coat and round black cap, carries a
German jagerrifle. In reality, the
Pennsylvania long rifle, deriv'd from the
jagerrifle, would be his weapon of choice.
   The Pennsylvania Infantryman wears a
brown coat faced white and canvas overalls.
The German origin of the illustration carries
through; note the long queue [pigtail] of hair,
common among German soldiers of the period.

universally recorded as "Captain Hains" due to a 1778 printer's error, was placed in command of the troops on the ground floor.[80] Men were assigned to cover each window and given orders to bayonet anyone who tried to get inside. Some men went into the basement; the rest dispersed to the upper floors.[81] A few even climbed out onto the roof.

The Preliminary Battle at Cliveden: 6:15 A.M.

The men of Captain Bower's company of the 6th Pennsylvania Regiment were jubilant. Pennsylvania and Maryland Continentals successfully thrashed the hated "bloodhounds" of the 2nd Battalion of British Light Infantry, driving them into ignominious retreat. In spite

FIG. 20b: Commander-in-Chief's Guard & a Contin ₐₗ Soldier, German Engraving, 1784

The Commander-in-Chief's guard, shown as a Dragoon of the 3ᵈ Continental Dragoons, in a white uniform faced sky-blue.

The Continental officer depicted wears very German style clothing: cocked hat with scallop edged lace, long queue and German cuffs.

of the 6th Pennsylvania's losses so far, the men pressed on. Private Philip Ludwig, a large Pennsylvania German from Reading, saw a handsome British musket leaning against a fence and exchanged it for his own.[82] As the line advanced, Ensign Charles Mackinett said to Lieutenant John Markland, "Here we are at Chew's house!"[83] When the regiment came within sight of the house, the muskets of Musgrave's British troops spoke. Markland said that the balls seemed to come in showers.[84] Private Ludwig, in the front of the advance, fell dead at the front gate, killed by a ball in the forehead.[85] Lieutenant James Glentworth was hit soon after, catching a musket ball in his right arm. Lieutenant Markland also was struck in the upper right arm, the ball splintering the bone near the shoulder.[86] Ensign Mackinett caught Markland as he fell.[87]

After firing a few volleys at the British inside Cliveden, the Pennsylvania troops moved on. Wayne's men passed behind the mansion and continued toward the main British camp in the heart of Germantown.[88]

Conway's men disengaged and marched off to the right, behind Sullivan's men, to form the extreme right flank of Sullivan's line. Sullivan's Maryland troops, on the west side of Germantown Road, also passed the house, abreast of Wayne's men.[89] Major John Eager Howard of the 4th Maryland Regiment was on the extreme left of Sullivan's line and was moving along the west side of Germantown Road. The regiment's commander, Colonel Josias Hall, had been knocked out of action when Major Howard's horse, which the colonel had borrowed, rode the colonel under a cider press near Mount Pleasant. With Hall injured, Howard took command of the regiment. He saw the two six-pounders abandoned by the British light infantry on the road near Cliveden. As his Marylanders advanced, Musgrave's troops fired on them without effect.[90]

A short lull in the fighting occurred once the Americans passed Cliveden. Colonel Musgrave took the time to give the men inside the house a short speech. He told them:

> That their only safety was in the defence of that house; that if they let the enemy get into it, they would undoubtedly every man be put to death; that it would be an absurdity for anyone to think of giving himself up, with the hopes of quarter; that their situation was nevertheless by no means a bad one, as there had been instances of only a few men defending a house against numbers; that he had no doubt of their being supported and delivered by our army; but that at all events they must sell themselves as dear as possible to the enemy.[91]

Interlude

The American Commander-in-Chief was concerned. He and his staff had followed behind Wayne's and Sullivan's troops on the Germantown Road and witnessed the fierce fighting against the British light infantry. Washington worried that there was no sound of battle coming from the far left which would have indicated the arrival of General Greene's column on Limekiln Pike, necessary for a coordinated general attack. As the troops in front of him advanced, he could only hope that Greene's force, the bulk of the army, would soon engage.

Behind General Washington's entourage was the *corps de reserve* commanded by General William Alexander, Lord Stirling. Within this reserve force were General Francis Nash's Carolina troops and General William Maxwell's New Jersey Brigade.[92] If

FIG. 21: William Alexander, Lord Stirling (1726–1783), Attribut'd to Bass Otis After an Engraving, ca. 1858

Maj.ʳ Gen.ˡ W.ᵐ Alexander of New Jersey claim'd his ancestral Scottish title of Lord Stirling even as he led his Continental troops. His reserves served under Gen.ˡˢ Maxwell & Nash. They repeatedly assault'd Cliveden's "massy walls."

necessary, these troops would reinforce Wayne and Sullivan.

In a chance occurrence that serves to remind how random and terrible war can be, a parting shot from one of the British Light Infantry's six-pounders went high. The ball passed over the Pennsylvania troops, sailed above General Washington and his staff, and descended along the side of Germantown Road near St. Michael's Lutheran Church. Before it fell to earth, it struck a sign post and ricocheted into General Nash's horse. The ball passed through the horse's neck and tore into Nash's left thigh. Continuing on, it struck Major James Witherspoon, an aide of General Maxwell, in the head. Witherspoon, the son of Princeton College President and signer of the Declaration of Independence, Dr. John Witherspoon, died instantly. Nash's horse fell dead with the gravely injured general caught partially underneath him. Nash's men gathered around but the brave general told them to keep moving, insisting that he wasn't seriously injured. When he was finally pulled from under his horse, his leg was all but detached. Aides made a litter out of poles and eventually carried him over twenty miles to DeHaven's house near camp.[93]

Meanwhile, General Nathanael Greene's column was late. As his troops were far to the left on Church Road, they had farther to march than either Wayne's or Sullivan's. Compounding this problem was that Greene's guide took the column on the wrong road.[94] Now, as dawn arrived and ground fog began to form, they could hear the sound of battle off to their right. As they reached Limekiln Pike, the column swung to the right toward the sounds of musketry and artillery. In so doing, they

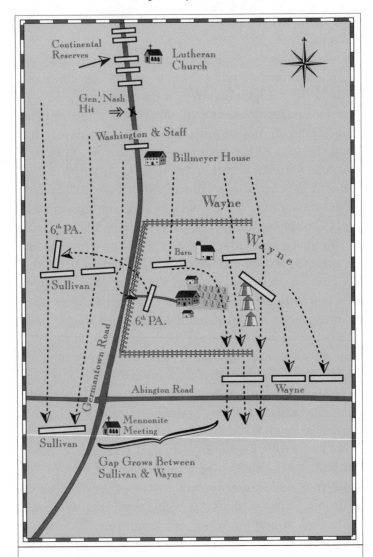

Continental
Reserves

Lutheran
Church

Gen.¹ Nash
Hit

Washington & Staff

Billmeyer House

Wayne

6.ᵗʰ PA.

Wayne

Barn

Sullivan

6.ᵗʰ PA.

Germantown Road

Abington Road

Wayne

Mennonite
Meeting

Sullivan

Gap Grows Between
Sullivan & Wayne

MAP 7. *Wayne & Sullivan Bypass Cliveden*
6:45 A.M.

headed straight for the pickets of Major Abercromby's First Battalion of British Light Infantry posted near Limekiln Pike and Abington Road.

Washington and his staff halted in front of the Billmeyer House at what is now the intersection of Germantown Avenue and Upsal Street.[95] Sullivan's, Wayne's and Conway's men pressed the attack, firing volley after volley at the enemy retreating into the fog and smoke. Each discharge of artillery and musketry added to the opaque atmosphere making visual contact nearly impossible.

Washington grew concerned with the expenditure of ammunition. Each man had been issued forty rounds before the battle; resupplying ammunition in the middle of an engagement was slow, difficult and dangerous. The Americans had not yet encountered the main British force, and Sullivan's troops were firing blindly into the fog at anything that moved. Fearing the waste of too much ammunition, Washington sent his chief aide, Colonel Timothy Pickering, forward to tell Sullivan to conserve his fire power.

Fig. 22: Col.$_{"}$ Timothy Pickering (1745–1829) by Charles Willson Peale ca. 1792

Pickering's anger over an inaccurate 1824 account of the battle led to two lengthy, detailed and indignant letters . . . and a goldmine of information on events at Cliveden.

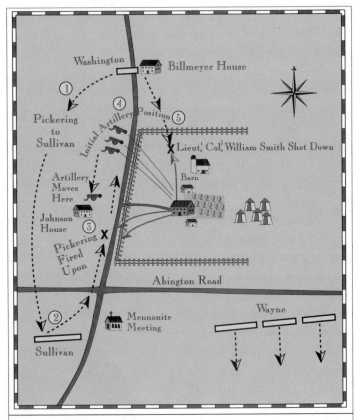

MAP 8. *Action Around Cliveden 7 A.M.*

①*Co.! Timothy Pickering takes orders from Washington to Sullivan.* ②*Pickering finds Sullivan "Near Mennonite Meeting," delivers message, and returns via Germantown Road.* ③*Passing in front of Cliveden, Pickering is fired upon & gallops out of range.*
④*Pickering sees artillery obliquely at Cliveden & orders them to move down & fire on the front of the house. He reports to Washington that British troops are in the house.* ⑤*After argument, L.! Co.! W.ᵐ Smith volunteers to take a flag of truce to Cliveden and is shot down.*

Pickering rode ahead through the fields and found Sullivan about five hundred yards away, his troops aligned near the Mennonite Meeting House. The colonel delivered Washington's order and quickly rode back up Germantown Road to the Commander-in-Chief.

A shot whizzed by Colonel Pickering's head as he neared the command position. Several others quickly followed. Instantly turning his head to the right, he saw a low stone wall along the side of the road. Behind it was a broad fine lawn ornamented with statuary. Up the lawn, about one hundred yards from the road, loomed an impressive gray mansion. Pickering could see gunflashes in the second floor windows, discharging a hail of lead in his direction. He spurred his horse and rapidly moved out of range. There were British troops in that house!

Further up the road he saw several American artillery pieces firing on the house at an oblique angle. Knowing the shots would have little effect from this position, Pickering ordered the artillery commander, Colonel Thomas Proctor, to

"*. . . At this time I had never heard of Chew's house and had no idea that an enemy was in my rear. The first notice I received of it was from the whizzing of musket balls across the road, before, behind, and above me, as I was returning after delivering the orders to Sullivan. Instantly returning my eye to the right I saw the blaze of muskets, whose shot were still aimed at me from Chew's . . . Passing on I came to some of our artillery who were firing very obliquely on the front of the house. I remarked to them that in that position their fire would be unavailing and that the only chance of their shot making any impression on the house would be by moving down and firing directly on its front . . . passing on, I rejoined General Washington who, with General Knox and other officers, was in front of a stone house . . . next northward of the open field in which Chew's house stood.*"

—Journal of Co^l_n Timothy Pickering

FIG. 23: Alexander Hamilton (1757–1804) by Charles Willson Peale, ca. 1791

Lieutenant Colonel Alexander Hamilton, Aide-de-Camp of George Washington, together with John Laurens and other aides urged Washington to post a regiment around Cliveden to hold the British in; Henry Knox's contrary advice led to the bombardment and attack on Cliveden.

move further down the road and fire directly on the front of the house. Pickering hurried on to inform the Commander-in-Chief of the situation at the house.[96]

Thomas Evans and John Bevery were privates in Colonel Musgrave's company of the British 40th Regiment of Foot. With the rest of the soldiers posted on the second floor of Mr. Chew's house, they stayed alert for movement outside. They fired shots at anything that moved, especially on Germantown Road. They sent a few shots at a horseman riding up the road away from the battle. It was comical to watch the horseman's reaction: first surprise, then quick motion to get out of range. A few minutes later, their grim amusement turned to consternation as they observed field pieces being unlimbered across the road, just out of musket range.

Fateful Decision

Logic dictated that a single regiment be posted around Cliveden to prevent the remnant of the British force from sallying out and creating chaos behind the American lines. Colonel Timothy Pickering and other young aides of General Washington, including Alexander Hamilton, supported this idea.[97] The Commander-in-Chief was inclined to agree until he heard the opinion of the only general present, his Chief of Artillery, Major General Henry Knox.

Knox was of the opinion that the house presented a real danger to the rear of the American army. Using the dictum that "it was unwise to leave a 'fortified castle' in the rear," he suggested that the position be "reduced" by cannon fire. While this choice of action was difficult to comprehend, his next order proved more incredible. He ordered that a summons for

FIG. 24: Maj.ʳ Gen.ˡ Henry Knox (1750–1806), Engraving Done 1782

Knox advised Washington that it was "unwise to leave a 'fortified castle' in the rear," resulting in the recommendation that Cliveden be reduced by cannon fire. He also urged that an American soldier approach the house with a summons for surrender. Both ideas proved disastrous for the Americans.

FIG. 25: Drawing, "Chew's House," Showing the Battle of Germantown, 19ᵗₕ Century

Most views of the Battle of Germantown show the house set in a clearing but with large trees to the rear. Period descriptions often note the classical statuary on the front lawn and a drive lined by cherry trees. See also Figure 9.

surrender be sent to the occupants of the house so that they could give themselves up before the Americans attacked.

Pickering was aghast. He argued that a summons at this stage of the battle would be ridiculous since the conflict was far from decided. Pickering held that the British troops in the house would fire on the flag, but over his objections and those of other aides, Washington decided to follow General Knox's advice.[98]

The Deputy Adjutant-General, Lieutenant Colonel William Smith of Virginia, volunteered for the dangerous duty of carrying the summons to the house. Accompanied by a drummer to beat the parley signal, he left the front

FIG. 26: *"Battle of Germantown"* *by* Xavier Della Gatta, 1780

While Cliveden's architectural details & the landscape resemble an Italian stageset more than reality, Della Gatta accurately portrays military actions & uniforms.

DETAIL 26a: *Lower left foreground: soldier carrying wound'd officer and officer on horseback rearing up. L.ᵗ Mansart S.ᵗ George, seriously wound'd in the head, is carried off to hospital by Private Peacock of the 52ᵈ Reg.ᵗ. Sir W.ᵐ Howe's horse rears up as artillery shots inform him that the American attack is not "a scouting party" as the 2ᵈ Batt.ⁿ L.ᵗ Inf.ʸ withdraws.*

DETAIL 26b: *Part of the 40.ᵗʰ Reg.ᵗ enters the house while another part fires over a fence to support the 2.ᵈ Batt.ⁿ L.ᵗ Inf.ʸ retreating.*

of the Billmeyer house and began to walk across the field toward Cliveden.[99]

Cliveden stood on a low rise of ground and commanded the area around it. Contemporary accounts describe the property as having expanses of open ground broken by a row of cherry trees lining a carriageway leading from Germantown Road to the house.[100] An open field about 150 yards wide separated Cliveden from the Billmeyer house.[101] Classical marble statues ornamented Cliveden's front lawn and to its rear was a fenced garden.[102]

The British soldiers on the second floor of Cliveden scanned the dark and hazy ground in front of them, alert for movement. Out of the northwest windows of the house they could see two figures approaching in the distance. Someone took careful aim and fired; one of the figures grabbed his leg and dropped. Other figures ran to the fallen man, picked him up and carried him away in the mist.

No British accounts mention an attempted parley. In all likelihood, the British simply fired at moving figures, as they had fired at Colonel Pickering riding up the road. Pickering states that a man could be clearly seen at 100 yards at this time in the battle.[103] Perhaps the British remembered the "no quarter" behavior of the Pennsylvania troops against the Light Infantry and gave this response. Whatever the possibilities, the result was that Lieutenant Colonel William Smith, Deputy-Adjutant from Virginia, had his leg shattered by a shot fired from Cliveden. American troops carried him back to the Billmeyer House and eventually to camp near Pennypacker's Mills [Schwenksville] where he later died.[104]

IX.

Phase III: Musgrave's "CASTLE" *under* Attack

❖ ❖ ❖ ❖ ❖ ❖ ❖ ❖ ❖ ❖ ❖ ❖ ❖ ❖

6:45 A.M., 4$_{''}^{th}$ October 1777.
Reduction by Cannonade:
The Artillery Bombardment

THE REDUCTION OF CLIVEDEN began with a furious artillery barrage. The Americans set four field pieces, ranging in size from three- to six-pounders, on the west side of Germantown Road about 120 yards from the front of the house. These guns, part of the Fourth Continental Artillery commanded by Colonel Thomas Proctor of Pennsylvania, were attached to General William Maxwell's New Jersey Brigade. Elements of the reserve, made up of Maxwell's troops and Nash's Carolina brigade, were also involved in the attack.

FIG. 27: Battle of Germantown,
Unknown Artist, ca. 1790

This oil painting was found in England in 1989 & purchased
by Cliveden. Its remarkable accuracy in detail, both in the
architectural elements of the house and in the troop location,
suggests that it was executed by an artist who had been on site
that fateful morning of October 4, 1777.

A thunderous bombardment began. The first shot blew the front doors off their hinges.[105] Solid shot slammed against the thick stone front walls, sending stone splinters and bone-shaking concussions through the air. Other shot burst through the wooden shutters and thudded into the plaster interior walls. Shot hit the front steps, sending stone chips flying in all directions. Some of the lawn ornaments were knocked to pieces; others lost arms, legs and heads.

DETAIL 27a: The Artillery fires at Cliveden on an oblique angle, the position in which Pickering found them; he order'd them to move to the right & fire directly on the front of the house.

DETAIL 27b: Maj.ʳ John White, aide of Gen.ˡ John Sullivan, attempts to set the northwest window of the house on fire; he was mortally wound'd by a shot from the basement window.

DETAIL 27c: Col.ˡ Thomas Proctor of Pennsylvania commanded the 4ᵗʰ Continental Art.ʳʸ. His four field pieces shower'd Cliveden with grapeshot and roundshot for nearly an hour.

DETAIL 27d: A prominent dying figure is surround'd by medical assistance. This may represent Gen.ˡ Francis Nash or, perhaps, Lieu.ᵗ Col.ˡ William Smith, both of whom were mortally wounded near Cliveden.

Inside the front hallway of Cliveden the world became a horrifying nightmare. As it was early on a foggy gray morning and the doors and window shutters were closed, the room was as dark as night. Then came the blast of cannons only 100 or so yards away, followed by the concussion of the shots hitting the walls. When the front doors suddenly blew off their hinges, a few of the men inside were wounded with stone chips which flew from the wall.[106] The dark hall filled with plaster dust, stone fragments, splintered wood and shattered glass, together with the gut-wrenching combination of terror and determination of veteran soldiers preparing to fight to the finish.

FIG. 28: "The Battle Germantown" by Edward Lamson Henry (1841–1919), *1875*

Samuel Chew III (1832–1887) commissioned New York artist E. L. Henry to paint a view of the Battle of Germantown to hang in Cliveden as a memorial to that fateful day. Executed in gray tones, the painting conveys the drama of the day at the expense of complete historical accuracy.

Captain William Harris of the British 40th Regiment, assigned by Colonel Musgrave to command the troops on the first floor, directed the men to try and rehang the doors as well as possible. He also ordered his troops to throw whatever furniture was available against the doors as a barricade. Soldiers piled chairs and tables against the shattered doors and awaited the onslaught of the Americans.[107]

FIG. 29: "Cliveden Entrance Hall During the Battle of Germantown," Study for an Unexecuted Painting by E. L. Henry, ca. 1875

This small study is almost ghostly in quality and presents a romantic view of the British occupation of Cliveden. In actuality approximately 30 soldiers were posted downstairs. The remainder of the 40$_{th}$, approximately 100 men, were posted on the second and third floors, and possibly the roof, all superior vantage points to pick off approaching Continental infantrymen.

Aside from chipping the walls and shattering the woodwork, the shot striking the front of Cliveden did little serious damage to the structure. The field pieces were simply too light to break down the cut-stone "massy-walls."[108] The Americans needed a new tactic to achieve their objective.

FIG. 30: Cliveden "battle doors" Display'd in Entrance Hall, Late 19th Century Photograph

Remarkably, Cliveden's original cannonball-battered front doors survived and were kept as relics. By the late 19th century the Chew family occasionally displayed them in the entrance hall of the house, enhanced by three muskets. Family tradition held that two muskets had been removed from the yard after the battle. Tragically a fire in Cliveden's carriage house destroyed the doors in 1970.

Reduction by Storm: The First Wave

The New Jersey Brigade, comprised of Colonel Matthias Ogden's 1st New Jersey Regiment and Colonel Elias Dayton's 3rd New Jersey Regiment, formed for action. As it became increasingly obvious that the artillery had little chance of smashing the walls down, the decision was made to try to take the house by storm and drive the British out with infantry. Such a tactic required courage and determination on the part of the attackers as they were about to face muskets aimed at point-blank range by a well-positioned opponent.

The artillery switched ammunition from solid shot to grapeshot. Grapeshot consisted of about twenty small iron balls packed in a linen bag, resembling a bunch of grapes. When fired, the shot scattered into a deadly iron hail. Effective up to 250 yards, grapeshot was murderous on closely-packed troops. The artillerymen aimed at the upper floors of the house to try and keep the British infantry down while the American troops approached the house.[109]

Colonel Elias Dayton, on horseback, led his 3rd New Jersey Regiment toward the house under the cover of grapeshot from Proctor's artillery. When they got close, the artillery ceased firing and the troops rushed toward the front door.

FIG. 31: Colonel Elias Dayton (1737–1807) Attribut'd to Joseph Sharples, S$_{\text{.}}^{\text{r}}$, 1795–1800

Dayton's 3$_{\text{.}}^{d}$ New Jersey regiment assaulted Cliveden "with great intrepidity, but were received with no less firmness." His horse was killed three yards from the northwest corner of the house. Dayton, Ohio is named in his honor.

The British 40th Regiment opened fire on the rebels at point-blank range. Jerseymen fell at a murderous rate. Colonel Dayton's horse was shot from under him three yards from the northwest corner of the house.

Some of the Jersey troops made it to the front door and tried to force their way in, only to be bayonetted by the determined men of the 40th in the front hall. With several men and officers left dead on the front steps, the attack was repulsed.[110]

Reduction by Fire: The Incendiary Attempts on Cliveden

A number of young staff officers decided to try and set Cliveden on fire. Lieutenant-Colonel John Laurens of South Carolina, one of General Washington's aides, accompanied by an intrepid French volunteer aide, the Chev.[er] du Plessis-Mauduit, took some straw from a barn and crept up to the north side of the house near the kitchen and attempted to set the windows on fire.[111] Two aides of General Sullivan, Majors John White and Edward Sherburne, also joined in the attempt to torch the house.

None of the attempts to fire the house succeeded. British soldiers stationed in the basement shot Major White as he tried to set the northwest window on fire. Sherburne's fate was equally

> *"If James can purchase a broad Green Ribband to serve as the Ensign of my Office and will keep an account of what he lays out for me in this way I shall be obliged to him—My old sash rather disfigur'd by the heavy Rain which half drown'd us on our march to the Yellow Springs [Sept. 16, the "Battle of the Clouds"], (and which by the bye spoilt me a waistcoat and breeches of white Cloth and my uniform Coat, clouding them with the dye wash'd out of my hat) served me as a sling in our retreat from Germantown and was rendered unfit for further Service . . . "*
>
> —*Lieu.[t] Col.[l] John Laurens, Aide-de-Camp to Washington*

grim. A British soldier bayonetted the American in the mouth as he attempted to pry open a ground floor window.[112] Lieutenant-Colonel John Laurens was injured in the shoulder as he attempted to set fire to the house. He made a sling out of his green aide's sash during the retreat.[113]

Du Plessis-Mauduit managed to pry open a window and mount the sill when a British officer appeared and pointed a pistol at him, demanding his surrender. A British soldier suddenly entered the room, saw du Plessis and fired hastily, striking the British officer by mistake. It is possible that the injured officer was Lieutenant James Campbell of Major Bradstreet's Company of the 40th who is known to have been wounded in defense of the house.[114] Mauduit closed the window, lucky to have escaped uninjured. He then faced the dilemma of staying relatively safe from British fire by remaining near

FIG. 32: Thomas Antoine du Plessis-Mauduit by an Unidentified Artist Possibly after Maurice-Quentin de la Tour, ca. 1900

The French Chev.ᵉʳ du Plessis-Mauduit served as a volunteer aide to Washington. He and John Laurens attempted to burn Cliveden but became trapped by gunfire against Cliveden's walls. Being a "true Frenchman," he risked death by walking away rather than ridicule by running.

staying relatively safe from British fire by remaining near

"... a fire of musquetry, which proceeded from a large house within pistol-shot of the street, suddenly checked the van of his troops. It was resolved to attack this house; but cannon were necessary, for it was known to be of stone, and could not therefore be set fire to. Unfortunately, they had only six-pounders: the Chevalier Duplessis-Mauduit ... resolved to attack by main force this house, which he was unable to reduce by cannon. He proposed to Colonel Laurens to take with him some determined men, and get some straw and hay from a barn, to set fire to the principal door ... M. de Mauduit making no doubt that they were following him with all the straw in the barn, went straight to a window on the ground floor, which he forced, and on which he mounted. He was received, in truth, like the lover who mounting a ladder to see his mistress found the husband waiting for him on the balcony: I do not know whether, like him too, on being asked what he was doing there, he answered, I am only taking a walk; *but this I know, that whilst a gallant man, pistol in hand, desired him to surrender, another less polite entering briskly into the chamber, fired a musquet shot, which killed, not M. de Mauduit, but the officer who wished to take him. After these slight mistakes, and this little quarrel, the diffi-*

the wall of the house or exposing himself to both gunfire and ridicule by running from the house. He chose to make a dignified withdrawal from the house and returned unscathed.[115]

Reduction by Encirclement: The Late Arrival of Woodford, 7:00 A.M.

General Greene's column, marching on the Limekiln Pike, encountered the pickets of the 1st Battalion of British Light Infantry and deployed for battle. Greene

culty for him was to retire. On one hand he must be exposed to a smart fire from the first and second floor; on the other, a part of the American army were spectators, and it would have been ridiculous to return running. Mr. de Mauduit, like a true Frenchman, chose rather to expose himself to death than ridicule; but the balls respected our prejudices; he returned safe and sound, and Mr. Laurens, who was in no greater haste then he,, escaped with a slight wound in his shoulder. I must not here omit a circumstance which proves the precarious tenure of a military existence. General Washington thought that on summoning the commander of this post he would readily surrender; it was proposed to Ms. de Mauduit to take a drum with him, and make this proposal; but on his observing that he spoke bad English, and might not, perhaps, be understood, an American officer was sent, who being preceded by a drum, and displaying a white handkerchief, it was imagined, would not incur the smallest risque; but the English answered this officer only by musquet shot, and killed him on the spot [sic]."

—*Marquis de Chastellux from*
Travels in North America, 1780–1782

placed Stephen's division on the right of Limekiln Pike while the rest of his own division deployed on the left side of the road. McDougall's brigade held the extreme left flank, and Woodford's brigade was on the extreme right. Once in place, this wing of the American line advanced, nearly forty minutes late in their arrival.

The 1st Battalion of British Light Infantry put up a good fight, but it was as hopelessly outnumbered as had been the 2nd Battalion. The 1st Light Infantry grudgingly withdrew into the fog with the Americans in pursuit. The American brigades passed over ground broken up by numerous creeks, woods and fences which caused

> " . . . *the left wing engaged, and both wings met almost in the same point, which was at Mr. Chew's house . . . this house of the Chew's was a strong stone building, having windows on every side, so that you could not approach it without being exposed to a severe fire; which, in fact, was well-directed . . . I am persuaded they [left and right wings] sometimes fired on each other, particularly at Chew's house, where the left wing supposed the cannon balls fired by the right wing at the house came from the enemy."*
>
> —*Col.*, *Timothy Pickering*

the troops to become separated and confused. Once in the fog and smoke, the brigades lost sight of one another.

Heavy cannon fire and musketry drew Woodford's Virginia Brigade, already on the extreme right of Stephen's division, even further to the right. As they advanced, with Abington Road on their left flank, they descended into a small valley. On the rise in front of them was an empty encampment next to a fenced garden with a large mansion flanked by two smaller outbuildings.[116] The sound of bombardment and musketry came from that area.

As the Virginians approached the house, gunfire erupted on them from the second floor. Occasional cannonballs and grapeshot flew out of the house and landed among the infantry. Woodford halted his men out of musket range and had his four artillery pieces unlimber and open fire on the rear of the house. Cannon fire tore off the building's back door.[117]

Eight artillery pieces now were firing upon Cliveden from opposite sides of the building. Some of the rounds passed over or through the house, landing among the American troops who surrounded it. With cannonballs flying from two directions, some men believed that the British were shooting artillery out the windows.[118]

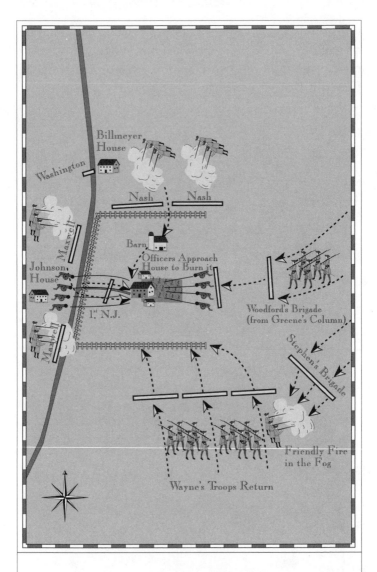

MAP 9. *Action around the House*
7:00–8:00 A.M.

X.

Mistaken Identity:
The Collision *of* WAYNE
and STEPHEN

7:30 A.M. 4ᵗʰ October 1777.

GENERAL ANTHONY WAYNE's Pennsylvania troops advanced several hundred yards beyond Cliveden toward the center of Germantown, driving the 2nd Battalion of British Light Infantry before them. When the artillery began to bombard Cliveden and Maxwell's infantry tried to storm the house, the Pennsylvanians could hear the sound of the engagement in their rear. They grew concerned that a major counterattack by the British might be occurring behind them. Since the fog and battle smoke had reduced visibility to near zero, they were unable to see what was happening. Wayne's right flank lost contact with Sullivan's men who

FIG. 33: Battle of Germantown,
Probably Early 19$_{"}^{th}$ *Century*

Photograph of an original work of art whose location
is unknown. This view shows the lane leading from
Germantown Avenue to Cliveden as well as toppled statuary
and casualties littering the lawn. This image likely is based on
the British medal struck in ca. 1785 to commemorate
the Battle of Germantown (see Fig. 34).

were several hundred yards to the right, somewhere in
the mist, engaging part of the main British force at a distance.

Some of Wayne's force began to countermarch back
toward the sound of the firing at Cliveden.[119] By doing
this they approached Cliveden from the south. Maxwell
and Nash already were hitting the house from the north
and west; Woodford's men were shooting at it from the

east. Wayne's approach would complete the encirclement of Musgrave and the British 40th.

As General Adam Stephen's troops moved southwest between Limekiln Pike and Abington Road, they lost contact with Woodford's brigade on their right. While the remainder of Greene's division drove the 1st Battalion of British Light Infantry from their camp, Stephen headed toward the main British camp.

Suddenly, in the smoke and fog, Stephen's troops encountered a battle line advancing in their direction. They halted, dressed the line, presented their muskets and fired a volley—right into Wayne's Pennsylvania troops who were countermarching toward the fight at Cliveden where they assumed a British counterattack was underway.

As they advanced through the battle smog, Wayne's troops saw a battle line formed off to their right. This line took aim and fired; obviously it was part of the "British counterattack" which was responsible for all the shooting behind the American lines. The Pennsylvanians halted, wheeled to the right and returned fire. Stephen's troops fired another volley which Wayne's men returned.

It is not known how long the exchange of fire between the American brigades lasted or how many casualties resulted. What is known is that the tragic mistake created a large hole in the American battle line. Sullivan's left flank was now uncovered and Greene's entire right wing was gone, leaving the left wing unprotected. Worse yet, the American reserves wasted themselves trying to dislodge a small number of troops from a well-defended position.

XI.

Retreat *and* Counterattack

8:00 A.M. 4ᵗʰ October 1777.

IN A LETTER TO THE *London Chronicle* published in January 1778, a British officer, describing the
battle at Cliveden, said of the Americans, "To do them
justice, they attacked with great intrepidity, but were
received with no less firmness."[120] Musgrave's men
repulsed several attempts by the Americans to enter the
house.[121] All efforts to dislodge the British 40th Regiment
of Foot failed. The regiment held together but suffered
considerable casualties. Private John Bevery and Private
Thomas Evans were killed that day. Drummer John
Goscock of Colonel Musgrave's Company received mor-
tal wounds and died the next day.[122] In all, three British
soldiers died and twenty-five were wounded, a loss of
nearly one-third of the men in the house.[123]

The American attack fell apart almost as quickly as
it began. No one knows just who started the retreat.

Some Continentals simply ran out of ammunition and, in calling for more, encouraged counterattack. Some forces found their flanks unguarded and deemed it prudent to withdraw. Some faced the brunt of the British counterattack and had neither the men, ammunition nor strength to hold the line. In some places, rumors of counterattack, outflanking and impending capture spread like wildfire, making the retreat unstoppable.[124]

Whatever the cause of the retreat, the effect was dramatic. After nearly three hours of heartpounding success, the American attack fell to pieces. It crumbled so fast that the British pursued cautiously, fearing an ambush. They had been astonished at how spirited the American attack had been, making its sudden collapse inexplicable.[125]

Some American troops never made it to the battle. The Pennsylvania militia on Ridge Road saw limited involvement, and the New Jersey and Maryland militias on Old York Road simply never arrived. Other troops, such as the 9th Virginia Regiment, made it to their goal at Market Square, only to be taken prisoner *en masse*.[126]

General Charles Grey's 3rd Brigade and General James Agnew's 4th Brigade led the British counterattack. They received support from Lord Cornwallis's grenadier battalions who had double-timed it to Germantown from Philadelphia.[127] The brigades formed into column to move north on Germantown Road at about 8:00 a.m. The Americans were retreating northward, passing through fields behind the houses on both sides of the road.

The effects of the battle and hasty retreat left the fields in a shambles. Crops were trampled and smouldering in places, parcels of dead and wounded soldiers lit-

tered the landscape, ruined and broken fences lay shattered by gunfire.

As the Americans fled, General James Agnew, leading the 4th British Brigade in counterattack, sat mounted
at the head of his brigade on Germantown Road. A dignified and kindly man, he passed in front of the Mennonite
Meeting House where some armed locals fired upon him.
Tradition holds that the Americans were told to "aim for
the star on his breast," the star-shaped Order of the
Garter which adorned his uniform coat.[128] The gunshots
mortally wounded Agnew. He was carried to a nearby
house where his life slipped away. His body was returned
to his headquarters at the Wister House, later named
"Grumblethorpe."

As General Grey's 3rd British Brigade advanced,
their fifes and drums announced to the 40th Regiment in
Cliveden that relief was on the way. The 44th Regiment
was the first to reach Musgrave's post.[129] The 40th was
jubilant! After a battle which seemed so desperate and
long, the rebels had retreated. Musgrave's men sallied
out of the house and joined in pursuit. They encountered
elements of Sullivan's division withdrawing up the west
side of Germantown Road. Part of the 4th Maryland
Regiment, commanded by Major John Eager Howard,
turned and fired at the 40th, striking one of their
officers.[130] The British then kept a respectful distance
and pursued the Americans cautiously.

XII.

AFTERMATH
of the Battle

NEARLY ONE YEAR after the engagement Benjamin Chew described his beautiful Georgian house as "an absolute wreck."[131] Had he seen Cliveden at the end of the battle, his reaction might well have been more graphic. The front and back doors were shattered, the windows broken, the roof pocked with holes. The interior walls and ceilings were peppered with musketballs and grapeshot, and there were large craters in the plaster where cannonballs had struck. Gunfire splintered much of the paneling and woodwork. On the exterior, scars defaced the cut stone of the front facade and the stucco-covered stone walls on two sides. One six-pound ball penetrated the rear wall by the stairway, and part of this same wall was "started," or partially caved in, by the artillery.[132]

The carnage inside and outside the house was dreadful. Captain Johann Ewald of the Hessian jagers visited the house after the battle and described the interior as

> . . . looking like a slaughterhouse because of the blood spattered around . . . I counted seventy-five dead Americans around the house, among whom were seven officers. Some lay in the front doorway under the pile of tables and chairs; others lay under the front windows.[133]

Another Hessian officer counted eighteen dead, including one officer, outside the front door alone.[134] These were men of the New Jersey brigade which lost a total of forty-six dead and wounded.[135] The American casualties at Cliveden also included men from Pennsylvania, Delaware, Virginia and the Carolinas.

The 40th Regiment also suffered heavy losses. The official count was four dead and thirty-two wounded, which includes those companies which covered the retreat of the Light Infantry. Among the casualties were three officers: Ensign John Campbell, Lieutenant John Doyle and Lieutenant Alexander Philip Forbes.[136] One report stated that the 40th lost two dead and twenty-six wounded inside Cliveden alone.[137] This figure agrees with Captain Ewald's estimate of nearly thirty British casualties in the house.[138]

In the entire battle, one hundred and fifty-two Americans were officially listed as having been killed, including some 30 officers. Five hundred and twenty-one were listed as wounded, and over four hundred were "missing;" an official loss of over 1000 American troops.[139]

The British gathered the American dead, aided by locals recruited to help. John Ashmead later reported that he saw 30 bodies buried in a pit northwest of Cliveden. Abraham and Jacob Keyser saw seventeen dead, including several officers, lying along the inside of Chew's front fence. These men were buried under a cherry tree. The Keyser brothers also saw a "fine, large soldier from Reading, dead at the front gate," who probably was Private Philip Ludwig of the Sixth Pennsylvania Regiment. Near the turn of the 20th century, a parcel of dead soldiers was discovered south of the house when Johnson Street was graded. Mary Johnson Brown Chew, then mistress of Cliveden, had the remains moved and reburied at the corner of Johnson and Morton Streets.[140]

The British also buried their dead near where they fell in battle. The loss of the royal army amounted to 535, the number killed being 70.[141] Private John Waites, of the Light Company of the 52nd Regiment, 2nd Battalion of British Light Infantry, died on Germantown Road on the south slope of Mount Pleasant behind his camp. He was buried alongside the road, clad only in his overalls, or long trousers. Paymaster returns of the 52nd Regiment deposited in the British Public Records Office list his name as the only member of the Light Company killed on October 4, 1777. In 1987, renovation work in the basement of the old Mount Airy post office uncovered a skeleton near the foundation wall. Close examination of the remains revealed four pewter buttons at waist level, two of which bore the number "52." The anthropological studies revealed a man who stood about 5 feet 6 inches tall, in his mid-thirties, who lived a "rugged existence," an excellent description of a British light infantryman. John Waites received a proper military burial, some 210 years after his death on that dark and terrible morning.[142]

Other participants in the battle can be traced. Lieutenant Martin Hunter went on to become a Lieutenant General in the British army. His friend, Lieutenant St. George, received serious wounds in the head in the opening volley of the battle. He was carried to the hospital and trepanned. Hunter witnessed the operation and remarked that St. George wore a silver plate over the hole in his skull for the rest of his life.[143]

Hessian Jager Captain Johann Ewald later became a general in the Danish army. He wrote several volumes on "partisan," or light infantry tactics, based on his experience in America. Ewald is a hero in Denmark and his portrait hangs in the Koningsburg Palace in Copenhagen.[144]

Lieutenant-Colonel Thomas Musgrave, who commanded the British 40th Regiment, received the congratulations of both the British army and the nation who looked upon him as a hero for his valiant defense at Cliveden. He also received a letter from King George III which saluted his exemplary service. Musgrave later became a Lieutenant General in the British army.[145]

A meritorious conduct medal was struck not long after the battle which commemorated the valor of the 40th Regiment at Cliveden. British army histories list this award as one of the earliest examples, if not the first example, of British battle medals. The enlisted men were issued medals of bronze while officers received silver medals mounted on a blue ribbon to be worn sus-

*FIG. 34: Battle of Germantown Medal
(Reverse) 19th Century*

*Medals awarded to the 40th Regiment had a hole drilled at
the top for a loop and ribbon. They generally were inscribed
with the name of the man to whom it was awarded.*

pended around the neck. Later examples of the medal
indicate that it was awarded to men of the 40th for more
than 100 years after the event. The medal depicts the
engagement at Cliveden on one side and the inscription
"Germantown 4 October 1777" on the other.[146]

American troops who participated in the Battle of
Germantown also left their mark. Major James
Witherspoon of New Jersey, killed by the same cannon-
ball which mortally wounded General Francis Nash, was
buried "in Philip Weaver's front lot," near where he fell.
At a later date, Witherspoon's brother and sister came to
remove the body and return it to Princeton. The corpse

The Battle of Germantown medal is significant in British military history as one of the first combat decorations awarded for heroism in a specific engagement. Colonel Musgrave commissioned the medal for the men and officers who were posted at Cliveden. The officers' medals were silver and worn around the neck on a blue ribbon. The obverse of the medallion shows a depiction of the attack on Cliveden. Because it is contemporary with the event, it incorporates the following accurate details: American artillery posted across the road; road lined with rail fences; two toppled statues off their pedestals; American troops in battalion formation firing a volley from the road; correct window placement, kitchen shown; scattered troops and casualties on the lawn.The only glaring inaccuracy is that the side wall essentially repeats the front wall.

was located in a grave with six others, but "was too decayed and offensive to bear such a removal . . . he was known from the rest, by the loss of part of his skull, and by being the only one wrapped in a blanket. The sister cut off a lock of his hair."[147]

General Francis Nash of North Carolina was carried "on a litter of poles" back to camp, some twenty miles away. John Fanning Watson reported, "I have learned from the sons of one DeHaven, that their father had assisted in carrying General Nash, who was brought into his house, and then taken two miles further to his brother's house, where he died,—having in his profuse bleeding for his country's good, bled through two feather beds before he died."[148] Nash died on October 9, five days after being wounded, and was buried with full military honors at 10:00 a.m. on October 10.

Lieutenant Colonel William Smith of Virginia, the Deputy Adjutant-General who attempted to carry the

---

*FIG. 35: Battle of Germantown Medal,
19th Century Restrike*

*Members of the 40th Regim^t who successfully defended
Cliveden receiv'd this special medal, ca. 1780. The 40th continued to award this medal for meritorious action through
the 19th century, further underscoring the significance of the
Battle of Germantown to the Reg^t. Samuel Chew III received
this restrike as a gift from Sir Canliffe Owens in 1884.*

---

flag of truce to Cliveden, was shot in the left leg. As frequently occurred with such wounds, infection set in, and
Smith died on October 23, nearly three weeks after the
battle.[149]

Major John White of Pennsylvania, the volunteer
aide on General Sullivan's staff, was shot from the basement of Cliveden while attempting to set fire to the
northwest window of the house. He was described as
". . . the finest looking officer in the service—his beauty

and dress had conferred on him the sobriquet of 'beau White'." He rode back with the army to Abram Wentz's house on Skippack Road in the company of General Forman of New Jersey and "a very young officer from Virginia, wounded in the shoulder [John Laurens?]." White was described by a lady who saw him as ". . . cheerful, and declined any bed or assistance." Hearing an alarm of possible British pursuit, the party rode six miles further to Schwenksville. The exhaustion of the ride, together with the wound, induced a fever from which John White died on October 10.[150]

Major Edward Sherburne of New Hampshire, also of General Sullivan's staff, ". . . was in the severest of fire for near two hours before he received the fatal wound which forced him from the field . . . he endured with great constancy the pains occasioned by his wound, and departed this life with a heroic firmness, which well witnessed the satisfaction he felt in suffering for his much injured country." The major "Died at the American camp, near Pawling's mill, this evening [October 5]."[151]

General Francis Nash, Lieutenant Colonel William Smith and Major John White are buried together at Towamencin Mennonite Meeting.

Private Abraham Best, who lost his leg in the opening fight at Mount Pleasant, was sent to the hospital at Reading. He survived his injury and in 1785 was awarded a pension of $5 per month for life for his services to his country.[152]

Lieutenant John Markland also went to the hospital at Reading. He did not lose his shattered arm but suffered the ill-effects of his injury for a long time. He underwent numerous operations, including one by an "intelligent farmer" with a penknife, to remove bone fragments. Markland was a charter member of the Society of the Cincinnati and became active in Philadelphia politics. He died in 1837 at the age of 82.[153]

Lieutenant James Glentworth recovered from his wound. He later became Surveyor of the Port of Philadelphia.[154]

Ensign Charles Mackinett returned to Germantown after the war and continued to run the Green Tree Tavern. Fifty-five years after the battle, he applied for a government pension. His memory failing, he enlisted the help of his two old comrades-in-arms, John Markland and James Glentworth, to attest to his pension claim. He was granted a pension of $320 per year and back pay of $960. His pension certificate was signed, ironically, by S. Chew, Esquire.[155]

Of all the participants in the Battle of Germantown, Major John Eager Howard of the 4th Maryland Regiment attained the most lasting attachment to Cliveden. Decorated by Congress for bravery in the Battle of Cowpens, he went on become Governor of Maryland (1788–91) and a U.S. Senator (1795–1803). President Washington offered him the post of Secretary of War in 1795, but he declined. Much of the city of Baltimore is built on land formerly belonging to him.[156]Howard married Peggy Chew, daughter of Benjamin Chew, on May 23, 1787. Among the guests was George Washington, then President of the Constitutional Convention.[157] After the Chew family reacquired Cliveden in 1797, Howard made many trips to Germantown to visit his in-laws.

XIII.
Postscript

And of Cliveden itself? Its interior stained by blood and battle smoke, its windows and woodwork shattered by shot, the plaster pocked by musketry and grape, the roof torn with holes, the mansion bore the scars of the conflict. But the thick stone walls still stood. Sufficient repairs were made so that the property could be rented in 1778. Then in 1779, Chew sold Cliveden to Blair McClenachan, a wealthy privateer. McClenachan sold Cliveden back to Benjamin Chew in 1797, and his descendants continued to live there until 1972 when it became part of the National Trust for Historic Preservation.

Visitors, curious to view the site of the dramatic events of the morning of October 4, 1777, came to Cliveden beginning that same day. Hundreds of officers and soldiers, including George Washington, also visited over the subsequent years. Even today the tradition continues at Cliveden. Here people discover one of Philadelphia's greatest eighteenth-century houses, see furniture and objects from America's past, and recall the events of that dark, foggy and terrible morning in 1777.

GLOSSARY of 18th Century MILITARY TERMS

from AN UNIVERSAL MILITARY DICTIONARY by Capt George Smith, 1779

BATTALION: an undetermined body of infantry in regard to number, generally from 500 to 800 men . . . Sometimes regiments consist of but 1 battalion; but if more numerous are divided into several battalions, according to their strength; so that every one may come within the numbers mentioned . . . Each battalion is divided into four divisions, and each division forms two platoons.

BRIGADE: in military affairs, implies a party, or division of a body of soldiers, whether horse, foot, or artillery, under the command of a brigadier . . . A brigade of the army is either foot or dragoons [mounted infantry], whose exact number is not fixed, but generally consists of three regiments, or six battalions. Brigadier, a military officer, whose rank is the next above that of a colonel; appointed to command a corps, consisting of several battalions or regiments, called a brigade.

COMPANY: in a military sense, means a small body of foot or artillery, the number of which is never fixed, but generally from 45 to 110, commanded by a captain, a lieutenant, and an ensign, and sometimes by a first and second lieutenant, as in the artillery. A company has usually 2 sergeants, 3 or 4 corporals, and 2 drums.

CORPS de Battaille: the main body of an army drawn up for battle, whereof the first line is called the van, the second the main body, and the third the body of reserve, or rear-guard.

DIVISION: of an army, are the number of brigades and squadrons [cavalry] it contains; of a battalion, are the several platoons into which a regiment or battalion is divided.

REGIMENT: is a body of men, either horse, foot, or artillery, commanded by a colonel, lieutenant-colonel, and major: each regiment of foot is divided into companies, but the number of companies differ; though in England our regiments are generally 10 companies, one of which is always grenadiers . . . Each regiment has a chaplain, quartermaster, adjutant, and surgeon.

—Smith, Capt George. An Universal Military Dictionary, *London: J. Millan, 1779. Reprint, Museum Restoration Service, Ottawa, Ontario, 1969*

Endnotes

1. Ernest Kipping and Samuel S. Smith, *At General Howe's Side*, p. 22 [hereafter called "von Munchhausen," after Friedrich von Munchhausen, the author of the journal translated by Kipping and Smith]. Von Munchhausen states in his journal on July 18, 1777, "A few days ago I had an opportunity to copy the following list of our embarked regiments and their strengths, including servants, laborers, and some washer-women with each company . . . Total (not including artillery and sappers) 16,498." With the artillerymen and sappers, the number would be between 17,000 and 18,000.

2. William J. Buck, "Washington's Encampment on the Neshaminy," *Pennsylvania Magazine of History and Biography*, Vol. I, 1877, pp. 275–284. Washington moved his army into Pennsylvania when he received word that the British were in the Delaware Bay, and scouts were sent to keep an eye on the British fleet. When the fleet left the Delaware Capes and put out to sea, the Americans had little idea of what Howe was up to. Washington kept his army in the area north of Philadelphia and did not learn until August 21 that the British were in the Chesapeake.

3. Both Howe and Washington attempted to conduct a "hearts and minds" campaign to win over the generally neutral population. On August 25, two days after the British landed at Head of Elk, Howe issued a proclamation which promised safety to those inhabitants who remained peaceably in their houses. He also offered amnesty to all rebels who took an oath of allegiance to the King before October 1.

   Howe's proclamation promised that "the most exemplary Punishment shall be inflicted upon those who shall dare to plunder the Property, or molest the Person of any of his MAJESTY's Well-disposed subjects." Nonetheless, plundering occurred with alarming frequency and Howe's attempt to reassure the civilian population failed miserably. The orderly books of the British army and many of the journals of British officers note the courts-martial and executions of a number of soldiers found guilty of plundering the local inhabitants in violation of Howe's repeated orders.

Washington encountered similar problems with the behavior of some of the troops under his command, notably the Pennsylvania troops and local militia regiments. There was much resentment against the Quakers and other pacifist groups who refused to take up arms; many of the Quakers were believed to be Tories and war profiteers. Ethnic considerations were also evident: many of Pennsylvania's soldiers were Scots-Irish Presbyterian Ulstermen who emigrated from Ireland in the 1760s. They were a tough, hard-fighting lot who despised pacifism, "foreigners" and Indians. See John André, *Journal of Major John André*, p. 38. See also *The Writings of George Washington from Original Manuscript Sources*, Vol. IX, 1933. Washington, D.C.: US Government Printing Office, pp. 199–200, p. 243, p. 268. See also *The Journals of Henry Melchior Muhlenberg*, Vol. III, 1958. Philadelphia, Pa.: Muhlenberg Press, pp. 74–81.

4. *PMHB*, Vol. IV, 1880, p. 121. Howe's official report to England concerning battle casualties at Brandywine is very questionable. Examination of primary accounts, such as Captain Ewald's journal, indicate severe casualties near Birmingham Meeting alone, to say nothing of Kennett Meeting and Chadd's Ford. Likewise, a paper which was claimed to have been captured from a British officer's tent at the Battle of Germantown states that British losses at Brandywine totalled 1,976. The correct figure most likely falls somewhere between the two extremes.

5. The number of effective troops on this campaign is difficult to pinpoint since there was a combination of regular Continental troops, state troops and state militias from Pennsylvania, Maryland and New Jersey. These men varied considerably in quality and dependability. See von Munchhausen, p. 65, note #5.

6. Between September 11 and September 25, rain occurred on seven out of fourteen days and nights. During this period, Washington's army crossed the Schuylkill on September 12, recrossed it on September 14 and crossed it again with floodwaters raging around the men on September 19. The torrential rain which began about midday on September 16 (causing the "Battle of the Clouds"), referred to by Captain John Montresor as an "equinoxial gale," was perhaps part of a hurricane or tropical storm. It lasted nearly 30 hours and caused the British army to halt. Washington's troops moved through it over flooded roads to Yellow Springs and Warwick Furnace, a 15–20 mile march. The last of the rain ended on the morning of September 18, but

the creeks and rivers remained swollen for a day or two afterward. For fuller descriptions, see von Munchhausen, and G.D. Scull, "The Journal of Captain John Montresor, July 1, 1777 to July 1, 1778, Chief Engineer of the British Army," and unpublished manuscript written by Captain Thomas Armstrong, British Orderly Book, September 15, 1777–October 3, 1777.

7. See André, von Munchhausen, and Montresor. Also, "The Massacre of Paoli," *PMHB*, Vol. I, 1877, p. 371.

8. Letter to Anthony Wayne from his wife Polly, ca. September 22, 1777, Anthony Wayne Papers, Historical Society of Pennsylvania.

9. James Hunter, *The Journal of General Sir Martin Hunter*. Edinburgh: The Edinburgh Press, 1894, p. 32.

10. Hunter, pp. 31–2.

11. Hunter, pp. 31–2.

12. *PMHB*, Vol. I, p. 312.

13. Two paintings by Xavier Della Gatta in the possession of the Valley Forge Historical Society depict these two soldiers. Both paintings were done in 1782 and it is believed that they were done for either Hunter or St. George. The events depicted are found in Hunter's journal.

14. Hunter, pp. 31–2.

15. The British first sent troops to seize the American "magazine" at Valley Forge on the evening of September 18. More troops were sent on the 19th and the entire army moved to the area on September 21, the morning after the Paoli Massacre. The camp stretched from the banks of French Creek [west end of modern Phoenixville] to Fatland Ford [modern Valley Forge Park]. On the evening of September 22, the British began to cross the Schuylkill at Fatland Ford, having earlier created a diversionary crossing at Gordon's Ford. The British marched to Norristown and camped on the east bank of Stony Creek from the Schuylkill near Swede's Ford to Germantown Road. See André, Montresor, von Munchhausen.

16. The Hessians who served in the Revolution were from two German states: Hesse-Kassel and Hesse-Hanau, two principalities located in central Germany in the vicinity of Frankfurt. The traditions of warfare in 17th and 18th century central Europe made life miserable for civilians unfortunate enough to get in the

paths of the contending armies of mercenaries. Plunder, confiscation and impressment were to be expected; wanton destruction of homes and fields, rape, and murder were common. Hessians were not the only German mercenaries serving in America. Troops from Anspach-Bayreuth, Waldeck, Anhalt-Zerbst and Braunschweig (Brunswick) were also hired by the British government. The only non-Hessian German mercenaries with Howe's army were a company of Anspach Feldjagers serving under Captain Johann Ewald. Feldjagers [literally "field hunters"] were riflemen who served in the same capacity as light infantry.

17. Joseph P. Tustin, *Diary of the American War: A Hessian Journal, Captain Johann Ewald*. New Haven and London: Yale University Press, 1979, p. 91. [henceforth "Ewald"]

18. von Munchhausen, p. 36.

19. von Munchhausen, p. 36.

20. John Fanning Watson, *Annals of Philadelphia*, Vol. I, Philadelphia: Lippincott, 1874, p. 51. The details of this description help to authenticate its veracity. The "refugee greens" were American Loyalists; "refugee" was a common term for them at the time. The emphasis on "*no* display of regimental colors and *no* music" is interesting, since armies carried the regimental flags furled and cased on the march. Likewise, music was rarely played on the march, except to occasionally pick up morale or impress the inhabitants of a town. Evidently, there was no desire to "impress" the residents of Germantown.

21. See von Munchhausen, André, Montresor. With the casualties at Brandywine and the nearly 2000 men sent to Wilmington on September 12 and 13, the British force entering Germantown was probably about 14,000 strong.

22. Watson, p. 54.

23. "Well-disposed" citizens were those who were Tories at best or at least neutral.

24. Armstrong, p. 2. See also von Munchhausen and Montresor.

25. Armstrong, p. 2.

26. Watson, pp. 51–2.

27. See André's map and description of the battle.

28. The term "flank companies" referred to the position which these troops occupied on parade. The position of honor was the right flank of the line, occupied by the grenadier company, while the left flank was occupied by the light company. The flanks were the "danger spot"of a battle line and were to be protected by the best men in the unit.

29. "Sept. 26th. At half past Eight this morning Lord Cornwallis with the two Battalions of British Grenadiers and Hessian Grenadiers, two Squadrons of sixteenth dragoons and artillery with the Chief Engineer, Commanding officer of Artillery, Quartermaster and Adjutant-General marched and took possession of the city of PHILADELPHIA." Montresor, p. 41.

30. Montresor, p. 43. The line ran parallel to modern Spring Garden Street and ended at "Fairmount," the site of the Philadelphia Museum of Art.

31. Armstrong, p. 23.

32. See Watson, pp. 40, 55. Also Elias Dayton, "Papers of General Elias Dayton," *Proceedings of the New Jersey Historical Society*, Vol. III, p. 187.

33. This information was given by the anthropologist's report as stated on the exhibit of the remains of the soldier found in Mount Airy under the old post office building in 1987.

34. Hunter, p. 32.

35. *PMHB*, Vol. I, pp. 373–4, note 5. Charles Cotesworth Pinckney, an American officer, confirms this deliberate harassment of the British picket posts: "Previous to the Battle of Germantown, every measure was taken to prevent the Enemy from supposing a serious attack was meditated, their Patrols were regularly driven in, & their picquets assaulted by the [American] light infantry & Cavalry for three or four nights previous to the attack." Manuscript letter from Charles Cotesworth Pinckney to Judge Johnson. Nov. 14, 1820, Chicago Historical Soc. p. 3.

36. The location of the 40th Regiment's camp has been verified by a number of primary sources as having been located *behind* Cliveden. Major André's manuscript map of the Battle of Germantown shows the 40th's position behind the house; his map of the position of the army on October 6, after the battle, also shows them behind the house.

John Eager Howard states: " . . . the fortieth regiment was encamped in the field, near the house. I have been at the house more than twenty times since, and have frequently been shown the place where he [Musgrave] was encamped, *back of the house near the summer house* [emphasis added]. I am confirmed in this opinion by a son of Mr. Chew's, who says that the people of the neighborhood to this day shew the place where he was encamped." Howard, having married Peggy Chew, certainly would have been back at the house frequently to visit his in-laws.

Howard's letter contains the following postscript, which is verified from the original book by James Wilkinson's *Memoirs of My Own Time*, published in 1816: "P.S. Since writing the above I have read the account of the action by Wilkinson who in his memoirs Vol. I, page 363 says, 'the 40th regiment was encamped three quarters of a mile in the rear of the light infantry, in a field of B. Chew, Esq., and *eastward* of his country seat' [emphasis added]. To which he adds the following note, 'This fact is derived from Capt. Campbell of that corps, who was wounded in defence of the house.'"

A letter to the *London Chronicle* written by "an English Officer serving with the Hessians in America, dated Philadelphia, October 10, 1777" states that " . . . he [Colonel Musgrave] immediately ordered his regiment to get into a large stone house (which had been his quarters) . . ."

The background of the portrait of Colonel Musgrave (Fig. 13) shows the 40th's camp next to an area enclosed by a paling fence with Cliveden in the background. In the distance, over Musgrave's right shoulder, is a cluster of houses and a steeple [Concord School House?], which would be the village of Germantown. From these facts, it may be reasonably concluded that the perspective of the painting is the *rear* of the house.

A number of subsequent histories of the Battle of Germantown contain maps based on a 1784 British map by Lieutenant J. Hills and published by William Faden. Hills's map shows the 40th in a position far across Germantown Road west of Cliveden. Indeed, if this map is taken as a faithful rendering of the position, the 40th was located on the rise west of Lincoln Drive above Wissahickon Creek. In such a position, they would have been of no use to the Light Infantry in a surprise. It makes no military sense, given the position of the British Army, to have put the 40th in that location.

Hills was not in the Battle of Germantown. He came to America about 1778 and drew a number of maps which were published by Faden. The date of the publication of this map, 1784, indicates that it was drawn long after the battle, perhaps as a composite map from other sources.

This is not the only case of a mapmaker's error being propagated over and over again. It was a map of the Faden series which mislabeled two hills near Boston, resulting in the "Battle for Bunker's Hill," when the action actually was fought on Breed's Hill.

37. Hunter, p. 18.

38. Watson relates an incident concerning Musgrave after the battle: "A.K. [Abraham Keyser] . . . had often seen Col. Musgrave, who defended Chew's house . . . He had been shot in the mouth, and had his face disfigured thereby, with a hole in his cheek." Watson, pp. 54–55. The engraving in the Cliveden collection (Fig. 13) was executed in 1797, when Musgrave was a Lieutenant-General and Governor of Tilbury Fort, an important fortification on the Thames River east of London. The original painting, executed in 1787, is in a private collection.

39. Ewald remarked after the Battle of Germantown that "the regiment had suffered a great deal in the campaigns." Ewald, p. 96.

40. Part of the 40th was inside Nassau Hall, the main Princeton College building, when the battle took place. This British position surrendered after a short artillery bombardment. It is ironic that this same unit would once more find itself besieged inside a stone building in the Battle of Germantown.

41. Quartermaster/Paymaster Muster Rolls of the 40th Regiment of Foot, Period of June 24–December 24, 1777. Public Records Office, Edinburgh, Scotland.

42. von Munchhausen, p. 22.

43. Quartermaster/Paymaster Rolls.

44. John Graves Simcoe, *A Journal of the Operations of the Queen's Rangers from the End of the Year 1777 to the Conclusion of the Late American War.* New York: Bartlett, 1844, p. 17.

45. Pickering wrote in a letter to the *National Intelligencer* in 1827: "With its [ie. Cliveden's] 'massy walls' Musgrave had probably become well acquainted while encamped in its neighborhood; and, as an able and experienced officer, knew it was proof

against the light field artillery . . . in other words, Musgrave threw his troops into that house, because he knew it was *tenable* . . ." *National Intelligencer*, January 5, 1827. John Eager Howard of the 4th Maryland Regiment, who later married Peggy Chew, also believed that the position was not chosen by accident: "I presume that General Howe, seeing the advantageous situation of the house, upon high ground, descending every way and cleared all around, posted Musgrave there, with orders to occupy the house, in case of attack. If he did, he certainly shewed his military judgment." John Eager Howard, "John Eager Howard's Account of the Battle of Germantown," *Maryland Historical Magazine*, December, 1909, p. 317.

46. Dr. Alfred Lambdin, "Battle of Germantown," *PMHB*, Vol. I, 1877, p. 371.

47. "Sept. 30– . . . The 42nd Regiment of Scots and the 10th Regiment of English under Colonel Stirling were detached late last night" and, "Oct. 3–Late last night we heard the following news: The 42nd . . . and the 10th . . . went down to Chester . . ." von Munchhausen, p. 38.

An American account notes, "Upon receiving intelligence that part of the enemy's force was detached for particular purposes . . . it was agreed in council that we should march the night of the 3rd instant . . ." Sullivan to Weare, Jared Sparks, *The Writings of George Washington*. Vol. V, New York: Harper and Brothers, 1847, pp. 463–4.

48. This is an optimistic maximum number since many soldiers were sent out on patrols, picket and foraging details. It does not, however, include those who were ill. A report to Hessian General von Ditfurth stated, "Had General Washington's attack been as well carried out as it had been planned, our army which did not consist of more than 5000 combatants would have been in a very critical position, for twelve of the strongest battalions were detached." From the Hessian Papers, "Letters to General von Ditfurth," Z. 196, Morristown National Historical Park Collection.

49. *PMHB*, Vol. I, 1877, p. 399. Also see "Diary of Robert Morton," in the same volume, p. 13. von Munchhausen states, "To alarm our garrison at Philadelphia, Washington, immediately after he started to attack us, had some 100 men of the militia show themselves on the other side of the Schuylkill . . . Lord Cornwallis,

who soon realized that these were feints, came flying to Germantown . . ." von Munchhausen, p. 39.

50. von Munchhausen states, "Everyone admits that Washington's attack was very well planned. He knew our exact positions through his very good spies." von Munchhausen, p. 39. Also see note 49, above.

51. *PMHB*, Vol. I, 1877, p. 399. The times stated by various accounts differ considerably. Colonel Walter Stewart says 6:00 p.m., as does General Smallwood. Pickering says that by 8:00 the troops were marching. This may be accounted for by the fact that the columns who had the furthest distance to cover needed the extra time to make a coordinated attack possible. The columns in which Stewart and Smallwood were present had the furthest distance to cover, as they were part of the extreme left flank.

52. *PMHB*, Vol. I, 1877, p. 399.

53. Armstrong, p. 31. This entry was made at the top of a clean page. Since the book is found in the Washington Papers, it is reasonable to conclude that the book was captured the next day when the camp of the 2nd Light Infantry was overrun.

54. Officer "B," Unpublished Manuscript, Sol Feinstone Collection of the American Revolution, Journal 1776–7. Pickering's Journal further confirms this near-collision: "I understand that ye guide of the left wing mistook the way, so that altho' ye right wing halted a considerable time, yet it attacked first, tho' later than was intended; that halt being occasioned by information from a [British] prisoner that half a battalion of ye enemy light infantry [see note 53] had the preceding evening advanced on the same road a considerable way beyond their picquet. It was necessary therefore to make a disposition to secure that party of light infantry that their opposition might not frustrate that principal design. Such a disposition was in fact made, but the enemy had retired about midnight to their camp." Manuscript of the Journal of Timothy Pickering, Essex Historical Society, Massachusetts, p. 21.

55. Officer "B," pp. 42–4.

56. Hunter, p. 33. It is interesting to note this incident, since Robert Morton tells us the day after the Battle of Germantown, "I went to headquarters, where I saw Major Balfour, one of General Howe's Aid de camps [sic], who is very much enraged with the people around Germantown for not giving them intelligence of

the advancing of Washington's Army, and that he should not be surprised if General Howe was to order the country for 12 miles round Germantown to be destroyed." *PMHB*, Vol. I, 1877, p. 15.

57. Officer "B," p. 42. Lieutenant General Archibald Robertson, Royal Engineers, wrote of this incident. "[October] 4th Saturday. At 4 in the morning Colonel Abercrombie came to our Quarters and told of a man taken by the Pickquet who said He was a Flanker from the Rebel Army coming to Attack our Camps. Got on horseback with Sir William [Howe] immediately." Robertson, p. 151.

Ewald's journal gives a remarkable account of a warning he received from a prominent Philadelphian, Dr. William Smith, Provost of Pennsylvania Academy [University of Pennsylvania], whose country house on Ridge Road was the site of Ewald's Jager outpost: " . . . he [Smith] asked me to take a little walk with him . . . He led me behind the camp, and when he thought no one would discover us, he addressed me with the following words: '. . . I am a friend of the States and no friend of the English government, but you have rendered me a friendly turn . . . You have protected my property. I will show you I am grateful. You stand in a corps which is hourly threatened by the danger of the first attack when the enemy approaches. Friend, God Bless your person: The success of your arms I cannot wish.—Friend! General Washington has marched up to Norriton today! . . .' I stood for quite a while as if turned to stone . . . General Howe answered this news with a 'that cannot be!'" Ewald, p. 92.

58. "Officer B," p. 43.

59. Morton, *PMHB*, Vol. I, 1877, p. 15. Also see the Pension Papers of Charles Mackinett. Revolutionary War Pension Papers National Archives.

60. Lambdin, *PMHB*, Vol. I, 1877, p. 400.

61. von Munchhausen, p. 38.

62. Howard, p. 314: "As we descended into the valley near Mount Airy, the sun rose, but was soon obscured." Hunter, p. 33: "At this time the day had broke about five minutes, but it was a very thick, foggy morning . . ."

63. Hunter, p. 33.

64. Hunter, p. 33.

65. Hunter, p. 34.

66. Markland, *PMHB*, Vol. IX, 1885, p. 107.

67. Hunter states, "On our charging they gave way on all sides, but again and again renewed the attack with fresh troops and greater force. We charged them twice, till the battalion was so reduced by killed and wounded that the bugle was sounded to retreat." Hunter, p. 34.

Markland says, "The action continued very heavy for some time, the enemy retreating until our troops had expended all their ammunition [40 rounds each?] . . . the American line again advanced, and after pressing the British very severely for some time, the brigade was halted . . . information was brought that the British had driven our troops on the left . . . [we] immediately advanced to the relief, and after some hard fighting the British were again forced to retire." Markland, p. 107.

68. Howard, p. 314.

69. Letter, Anthony Wayne to his wife, ca. October, 6, 1777, Anthony Wayne Papers.

70. This assertion is conjectured based on circumstantial evidence. Ewald, who was in another part of the field [the Jager post at the Wissahickon on Ridge Road] says, "General Howe, who was awakened by the enemy cannonballs striking his headquarters, hurried to the army." Ewald, p. 93. This is translated from German. It is unlikely that this occurred as Stenton was so far away. However, the *sound* may have awakened him. This, too, seems unlikely, as it was reveille anyway.

Captain von Munchhausen, Howe's aide, was carrying a message to Lord Cornwallis "At my General's request," when he heard the shots at 5:30 a.m. Unless the request was made the previous night, it would presume that Howe already was up and working that morning.

General Robertson says, "At 4 in the morning Colonel Abercrombie [of the 1st Battalion Light Infantry] came to our quarters and told of a man Taken by the Picquet . . . Got on horseback with Sir William *immediately*."

What is certain is that Howe and his staff were on Germantown Road north of Cliveden as the Light Infantry retreated from Mount Pleasant. Both von Munchhausen and Hunter confirm this with their statements.

71. Hunter, pp. 34–5.

72. von Munchhausen, p. 38. In reality, the British light infantry had fled at least once before. At Breed's Hill in Massachusetts, the first pitched battle of the Revolution, they fled in the face of John Stark's New Hampshire troops. This initial setback thwarted Howe's plan to take the rebel position by a quick flanking movement. However, the British went on to win the battle when the Americans ran out of ammunition.

73. Hunter, pp. 34–5.

74. Hunter, pp. 34–5.

75. von Munchhausen, p. 38.

76. Howard, p. 315; General Henry Miller, "A Memoir of General Henry Miller," *PMHB*, Vol. XII, 1888, p. 427.

77. Letter, Sullivan to Weare, appearing in Sparks, p. 59.

78. "Extract of a Letter from an English Officer Serving With the Hessians in America, dated Philadelphia, October 10, 1777, *London Chronicle*, January 3–6, 1778.

79. There is some question about just how many companies of the 40th Regiment actually went into Cliveden. The usual number stated is six companies, but the number of men cited is between 100 and 120. The muster rolls of the 40th at this time averaged about 30 men per company. Captain Johann Ewald stated that only three companies went into the house and that there were no more than 100 men inside. While it is quite possible that the regiment on this given morning was severely understrengthed with men on picket duty and had 20 or fewer effective men per company, it is also possible that only three companies did in fact enter the house. Until the daily morning reports become available, the question will remain. What is clear, is that only part of the 40th went into Cliveden and that they numbered no more than 120.

80. *London Chronicle*. The double "r" and "i", written in the cursive script of the late 18th century, may be easily misread as a number of different letters. In this case the printer read "Hains" instead of "Harris."

81. *London Chronicle*; also James Wilkinson, *Memoirs of My Own Times*. pp. 364–5.

82. Markland, p. 108.

83. Captain Markland's Deposition, Pension Papers of Charles Mackinett, 1833.

84. Markland, p. 108.

85. Markland, p. 108. Also Watson, p. 52.

86. Markland, p. 108.

87. Pension Papers of Charles Mackinett, 1833.

88. At this stage of the battle, Wayne's and Sullivan's divisions lost contact with each other. Conway's men were ordered to fall in behind Sullivan and move down to the extreme right flank where they initially were assigned. This move, combined with the fog and numerous fences, caused the forces to lose contact and become broken in formation. See Sullivan's letter to Weare appearing in Sparks, p. 465.

89. Sparks, p. 465.

90. Howard, p. 315.

91. *London Chronicle*, January 3–6, 1778.

92. *PMHB*, Vol. I, 1877, pp. 394–5.

93. *PMHB*, Vol. I, 1877, pp. 394–5. See also Watson, p. 60.

94. Extract from the Journal of Timothy Pickering in Commager and Morris, *The Spirit of Seventy Six.* p. 626.

95. Pickering's Letter to the *North American Review*, published in *The National Intelligencer*, January 1827.

96. Pickering's Letter. A controversy erupted in the mid-1820s when a book entitled *The Life of Greene* by Judge William Johnson cast aspersions on the conduct of General Washington at Germantown. Timothy Pickering was so incensed at the accusations, which were based on faulty information, that he and other officers, including Henry "Light-Horse Harry" Lee, wrote refutations and had them published. The first chapter of Henry Lee's book *The Campaign of 1781* in the Carolinas is devoted to critical review of Johnson's work.

    Pickering wrote two letters in response to Johnson's book. The first is widely quoted in works dealing with the Battle of Germantown, as it gives a careful account of what Pickering saw. The second letter, 17 pages long in manuscript form, contains a "fact-by-fact" refutation and criticism of Johnson's inaccuracies. It is thanks to Pickering's obvious anger over this publication that we have another splendid account: that of John Eager Howard. It appears that Pickering wrote to Howard and asked for his account of what happened to support the refutations of Johnson's work.

97. Pickering's Letter. Pickering took particular offense at Johnson's description of the incident: "Here was presented the scene which Judge Johnson pronounces 'almost ludicrous!' 'One would suppose (says he) that Gen. Washington stood almost stupefied on the occasion, listening with deference to every *babbler* who chose to obtrude his opinions. 'He goes on—'Even field officers [did the judge mean that these were the *babblers*? or of a class still inferior?] '*Even* field officers are supposed to have forced their way into the circle of his legitimate counsellors; and the opinion [opinions] of some stand recorded in commemoration of *their* correctness and *his* folly.'"

98. Pickering's Letter. See also Henry Lee, *Memoirs of the War in the Southern Department of the United States*. New York: University Publishing Company, 1869, p. 96, and Colonel Benjamin Tallmadge, *Memoir of Colonel Benjamin Tallmadge*. New York: Thomas Holman, 1858, p. 23.

99. Pickering's Journal in Commager and Morris, p. 627; François Jean, Marquis de Chastellux, *Travels in North America*, Volume I, London, 1786, p. 213; Wilkinson, pp. 364–65.

100. Watson, p. 52.

101. Pickering's, Letter.

102. The remains of four full-length classical statues survive at Cliveden. There are also two marble lions flanking the front door, two classical marble busts mounted on pedestals, a marble "birdbath," the remains of five stone roof urns and pieces of what may be a sixth urn. Finally, there are two marble pedestals located behind the house, one of which matches the three pedestals in front of the building.

Of the four surviving statues, only one remains in the front of the house. It is missing both arms and the head has been reattached. Two other statues stand behind the house, minus their heads and arms, and in one case, a leg. The fourth statue's torso is wedged into the crotch of a catalpa tree near the other two statues; the base of a statue, probably belonging to the torso, is located near the cellar doors.

The pieces of a sixth urn are deposited at the base of a large sycamore tree near the kitchen dependency. These objects collectively have been on the lawn as described for as long as any member of the Chew family remembers.

There are two contemporary renditions of the Battle of Germantown which show these ornaments. However, the depictions are evidently based on descriptions rather than eyewitness observation by the artist. Other blatant errors in the renderings of detail may cast doubt on the credibility of source. Nonetheless, they are worth examining.

Xavier Della Gatta's painting of the Battle of Germantown, painted in 1780 (Fig. 26), shows Cliveden as a small box-like structure. Two full statues are flanking the house; the figure in full view is mounted upon a pedestal. The roof is flat, with busts on the front corners and urns on the back corners. The door and window arrangement on the house is accurate on the front.

The second rendition is found on the battle medal issued to the 40th Regiment (Fig. 35). On the front lawn of the house are two pedestals with the statues knocked down. The window arrangement on the front of the house is accurate, but the roof depiction on the side of the building is a repeat of the front.

The translator of Chastellux wrote in a footnote: "In 1782 I visited and passed a very agreeable day at this celebrated stone house . . . and saw . . . two or three mutilated statues which stood in front of it." [p. 210–11] Whether he refers to the full-length statues only or all the statues collectively is a matter of interpretation. For what it is worth, the classical busts and lions exhibit no signs of damage, though the pedestals are chipped. The full-length statues, on the other hand, are all seriously "mutilated."

See the portrait of Colonel Musgrave (Fig. 13) for an artist's rendition of the rear of Cliveden.

103. Pickering's Letter.

104. He is variously referred to as Lieutenant Smith or Captain Smith; at the time he died he was one of Washington's aides (Deputy Adjutant-General) with the brevet rank of Lieutenant Colonel. Pickering, the Adjutant General at the time, always refers to him as Lieutenant-Colonel. He was commissioned a second lieutenant of the 15th Virginia Regiment November 21, 1776, and promoted to first lieutenant July 4, 1777. F. B. Heitman, *Historical Register of Officers of the Continental Army*, Washington, D.C., 1893.

105. *London Chronicle*, January 3–6, 1778; *PMHB*, Vol. IV, 1881, p. 113; also, Officer "B," p. 45.

•106. *London Chronicle*.

107. *London Chronicle*. See also Ewald, p. 96.

108. Pickering's Letter.

109. *London Chronicle*.

110. Dayton, *PNJHS*, Vol. III, p. 185. ". . . the General [Washington] said . . . I have already directed the army to file off to the right and left, & ordered Col. Ogden[1st New Jersey Regiment] to remain with his regiment to watch the House, and to fall on the soldiers in it if they attempted to quit it."—Pinckney letter, page 6.

111. Chastellux, p. 213.

112. Morton, p. 14; Watson, pp. 49–50; Sparks, p. 466; White's obituary, *PMHB*, Vol. 20, 1896; Howard, p. 317.

Major White's activity in this situation is documented; Major Sherburne's is based on tradition. A source which cannot be documented stated that Sherburne was bayonetted in the mouth and that he walked back with the army to Schwenksville. Robert Morton's diary states, "One of the Americans went up to a window of the N. side of the house to set fire to it, and just as he was putting the torch to it he rec'd a Bayonet thro. his mouth, which put an end to his existence." Whether or not this was Sherburne cannot be determined. Sherburne is buried on the front lawn of the Pennypacker House, which served as Washington's headquarters after the battle.

It is puzzling that two of General Sullivan's aides would be detached from his staff at so critical a time, as Sullivan had passed Cliveden and was quite a distance away while this was occurring.

113. Chastellux, p. 213. Also, Lieutenant Colonel John Laurens, Letter to Henry Laurens, November 6, 1777, Laurens Papers, South Carolina Historical Society. Also see Wilkinson, pp. 364–5.

Wilkinson says, "Colonel Laurens, an aide-de-camp of General Washington, attempted with a party to force the main door." Chastellux states that "Mr. Laurens . . . escaped with a slight wound in his shoulder." The exact injury sustained is unclear; the fact that he made a sling might indicate a dislocated shoulder or fractured bone; there is no evidence of a gunshot wound or bayonet stab.

114. Wilkinson, pp. 364–365.

115. Chastellux, p. 213.

116. John Marshall, *The Life of George Washington.* Volume II, Fredericksburg, Va.: The Citizens' Guild, 1926, p. 323. Also see Musgrave's portrait (Fig. 13), which depicts his regiment's camp with a fenced-in area next to it; Cliveden sits on a rise in the background. André says, in an unpublished manuscript from the files of the National Army Museum in London, that the 40th Regiment "maintain'd themselves in a house strewing the yard, garden, avenue, etc. with a prodigious number of Rebel dead."

117. "Officer B," p. 45; Gerhard A. Uhlendorf and Edna Vosper, *Letters of Major Baurmeister to Colonel von Jungkenn Written During the Philadelphia Campaign 1777–78*, p. 24.

118. See Commager, p. 628. Several accounts mention the confusion and the idea that there was artillery inside the house. A letter by General John Armstrong refers to "wall pieces," which were large muskets also known as "amusettes." The Hessian jagers carried them as light artillery; it is possible that the British light infantry and the 40th Regiment may have had one or two with them. These weapons, firing projectiles weighing up to one-and-one-half pounds, qualify as light artillery.

119. Letter from Anthony Wayne, cited in J. Thomas Scharf and Thompson Wescott, *History of Philadelphia*, 1884, p. 358; Sullivan to Weare, Sparks, p. 466.

120. *London Chronicle.*

121. Marshall, p. 323.

122. Quartermaster/Paymaster Rolls.

123. Ewald states that, "During the battle some thirty men were killed and wounded." The report to General von Ditfurth states, "The 40th Regiment had 2 dead and 26 wounded." Ewald, p. 96; Ditfurth Letter, p. Z 205.

124. Sullivan to Weare, Sparks, p. 466.

125. General Smallwood wrote, "The retreat commenced . . . in the midst of victory at a time when no person could account for it, nor can the cause of it be yet ascertained . . . The enemy themselves are amazed and at a loss to account for the retreat . . ."

Lambdin, p. 402. British accounts attribute the cautious pursuit to the fog and lack of coordination of their forces pursuing an enemy over a wide area.

126. Sullivan to Weare, Sparks, p. 466.

127. von Munchhausen stated, "Lord Cornwallis . . . came flying to Germantown." [p. 39] General Howe wrote, "The grenadiers from Philadelphia, who, full of ardor, had run most of the way to Germantown . . ." [p. 331] John Fanning Watson reported that a civilian named John Smith "ran to Nicetown . . . and there met the British coming out from the city in a kind of half-running march." [p. 54]

128. Watson, p. 38. The tradition may be erroneous; Agnew possessed no known decorations. Alexander Andrew, General Agnew's servant, wrote to the general's wife in March, 1778: ". . . a party of the enemy, about 100, rushed out from behind a house . . . the general being then in the street, and even in front of the picquet, and all alone, [with] only me, he wheeled around, and putting his spurs to his horse, and calling to me, he received a whole volley from the enemy. The fatal ball entered the small of his back, near the back seam of his coat, right side, and came out a little below his left breast. Another ball went through and through his hand. I at the same instant, received a slight wound in the side . . . When he came [to] he could only turn his eyes . . . The doctor and Major Leslie just came in time enough to see him depart this life . . . about 10 or 15 minutes after he received the ball." Benson J. Lossing, *The Pictorial Field-Book of the Revolution*. Vol. II, New York: Harper and Brothers, 1860, p. 113.

129. André, p. 55.

130. Howard, p. 315.

131. Letter, Benjamin Chew, July 1778. Chew Family Papers, HSP.

132. Wilkinson, p. 365.

133. Ewald, p. 96.

134. Letter to General Ditfurth, p. Z. 205.

135. Dayton, *PNJHS*, Vol. III, p. 185.

136. Quartermaster/PaymasterRolls.

137. Two soldiers died on the day of the battle; the drummer, mortally wounded, died the following day. Chew family tradition holds that only one soldier actually died in the house during the

battle, in the northwest chamber on the second floor. Watson states that the Keyser brothers, visiting the house after the battle, "saw only one man who had been wounded in the house, and he was dying." [Watson, p. 53.] These accounts complement one another and coincide with the casualty reports, making the tradition quite plausible.

138. See note 123.

139. Lossing, p. 112n.

140. Watson, p. 52. Also see Markland, p. 108.

141. Gordon, p. 324. Gordon has a curious footnote regarding British casualties: "When the royal army quitted Germantown, the Americans found in one of the chimney hearths, some papers torn into pieces . . . and found them to be the returns of killed and wounded . . . amounting to about 800."

142. An exhibit of this discovery was prepared by the University of Pennsylvania and is currently (1994) in the possession of the Germantown Historical Society.

143. Hunter, p. 32.

144. Ewald, Frontispiece and Introduction.

145. The engraving of Musgrave's portrait (Fig. 13) which is in the collection at Cliveden was made in 1796. It states Musgrave's title as "Lieutenant General" and "Governor General of Gravesend and Tilbury Fort."

146. B. R. Mullaly, *The South Lancashire Regiment*, Bristol: The White Swan Press, n.d., p. 37.

147. Watson, p. 59.

148. Watson, p. 60.

149. Lambdin, p. 382.

150. Watson, p. 60.

151. Frank Moore, *Diary of the American Revolution from Newspapers and Original Documents*, Vol. I, New York: Charles Scribner, 1860. p. 506.

152. "Pennsylvania Pensioners of the Revolution," *PMHB*, Vol. XLII, 1918, p. 42.

153. Markland, p. 102.

154. Markland, p. 108.

155. Pension Papers of Charles Mackinett.

156. *Dictionary of American Biography*, John Eager Howard.

157. "Wednesday, 23 May, 1787— . . . dined at Mr Chew's with the wedding guests (Col. Howard of Baltimore having married his daughter Peggy). Drank Tea there in a very large circle of ladies." *The Diaries of George Washington*, Edited by John Fitzpatrick, Vol. III. New York: Houghton Mifflin, 1925, p.233. This wedding would have been at Chew's townhouse, Cliveden then being owned by Blair McClenachan. Washington visited Cliveden later that same year [August 19] while on a trip to Whitemarsh.

Bibliography

André, John, *Journal and Maps*. Boston: Bibliophile Society, 1903.

André, John, *Journal of Major John André*. Tarrytown:, N.Y.: William Abbat, 1930.

André, John, Unpublished Manuscript, National Army Museum, London.

Armstrong, Thomas, British Orderly Book, September 15, 1777–October 3, 1777, A.D., one volume, 16, 64th Regiment Light Infantry Company, Washington Papers, Library of Congress.

Buck, William J. "Washington's Encampment on the Neshaminy," *Pennsylvania Magazine of History and Biography*. Vol. I, 1877, pp. 275–284.

Chew Family Papers, Historical Society of Pennsylvania

Coombs, Thomas, Unpublished Manuscript Weather Journal, March 1777–May 1778, American Philosophical Society.

Francois Jean, Marquis de Chastellux, *Travels in North America*. Volume I, London, 1786.

Commager, Henry Steele, and Richard B. Morris, *The Spirit of Seventy-Six*. 2 volumes, New York: Doubleday and Company, 1958.

Cresswell, Donald H., *The American Revolution in Drawings and Prints: A Checklist of 1765–1790 Graphics in the Library of Congress*. Washington, D.C.: Library of Congress, 1975.

Dawson, Henry B., *Battles of the United States*. Volume I, New York: Privately published, 1860.

Dayton, Elias, "Papers of General Elias Dayton," *Proceedings of the New Jersey Historical Society*. Volume 9, 1857.

Dictionary of American Biography. Vol. 5, New York: Charles Scribner's Sons, 1933.

Drinker, Elizabeth, "Extracts from the Journal," *Pennsylvania Magazine of History and Biography*. Volume XIII, 1889.

Gordon, William, *The History of the Rise, Progress and Establishment of the Independence of the United States of America*. Volume II, New York: Samuel Campbell, Second American Edition, 1794, pp. 234–235.

Heitman, F.B., *Historical Register of Officers of the Continental Army*. Washington, D.C., 1893.

Hessian Papers, "Letters to General von Ditfurth," Z. 196, Morristown National Historical Park Collection.

Howard, John E., "John Eager Howard's Account of the Battle of Germantown," *Maryland Historical Magazine*. Volume 4, December 1909.

Hunter, James, *The Journal of General Sir Martin Hunter*. Edinburgh: The Edinburgh Press, 1894.

Kipping, Ernest, and Samuel S. Smith, *At General Howe's Side*. Monmouth Beach, N.J.: Philip Freneau Press, 1974.

Lacey, John, "Memoirs of Brigadier General John Lacey," *Pennsylvania Magazine of History and Biography*. Volume XV, 1901, pp. 105–106.

Lambdin, Dr. Alfred, "Battle of Germantown," *Pennsylvania Magazine of History and Biography*. Volume I, 1877, pp. 368–403.

Lossing, Benson J., *The Pictorial Field-Book of the Revolution*. Volume II, New York: Harper and Brothers, 1860.

Mackinett, Charles, Revolutionary War Pension Papers, National Archives, 1833.

Markland, John, Captain Markland's Deposition, Pension Papers of Charles Mackinett, Revolutionary War Pension Papers, National Archives, 1833.

Marshall, John, *The Life of George Washington*. Volume 2, Fredericksburg, Virginia: The Citizen's Guild, 1926.

Miller, Henry, "A Memoir of General Henry Miller," *Pennsylvania Magazine of History and Biography*. Volume XII, 1889, pp. 426–427.

Moore, Frank, *Diary of the American Revolution from Newspapers and Original Documents*. Vol. I, New York: Charles Scribner, 1860.

Morton, Robert, "Diary of Robert Morton," *Pennsylvania Magazine of History and Biography*. Volume I, 1877, pp. 1–39.

Mullaly, B.R., *The South Lancashire Regiment*. Bristol: The White Swan Press, n.d.

Officer "B," Unpublished Manuscript Journal, Sol Feinstone Collection of the American Revolution, 1776–77.

Pickering, Timothy, Letter, *North American Review*. October 1826, published in the *National Intelligencer*, January 1827.

Potts, William J., "Battle of Germantown from a British Account," *Pennsylvania Magazine of History and Biography*. Volume XI, 1887, pp. 112–114.

Quartermaster/Paymaster Muster Rolls of the 40th Regiment of Foot, Period of June 24–December 24, 1777. Public Records Office, Edinburgh, Scotland.

Robertson, Archibald, *Archibald Robertson, Lieutenant General of Royal Engineers, His Diaries and Sketches in America*. Reprint, New York: Arno Press, 1971.

Scharf, J. Thomas and Thompson Westcott, *History of Philadelphia*. Volume I, Philadelphia: L.H. Everts & Co., 1884.

Scull, G.D., "The Journal of Captain John Montresor, July 1, 1777 to July 1, 1778, Chief Engineer of the British Army," *Pennsylvania Magazine of History and Biography*. Volumes V and VI, 1881 and 1882.

Simcoe, John Graves. *A Journal of the Operations of the Queen's Rangers from the End of the Year 1777 to the Conclusion of the Late American War*. New York: Barlett, 1844.

Sparks, Jared, *The Writings of George Washington*. Volume V, New York: Harper and Brothers, 1847.

Tallmadge, Benjamin, *Memoir*. New York: Thomas Holman, 1858.

Tustin, Joseph P. *Diary of the American War: Hessian Journal of Captain Ewald*. New Haven & London: Yale University Press, 1979.

Uhlendorf, Gerhard A. and Edna Vosper, *Letters from Major Baurmeister to Colonel von Jungkenn Written During the Philadelphia Campaign*. Philadelphia: Historical Society of Pennsylvania, 1937.

Watson, John Fanning, *Annals of Philadelphia, 3rd edition*. Volumes I–III, Philadelphia: Lippincott, 1874.

Wayne, Anthony, Anthony Wayne Papers, Historical Society of Pennsylvania.

Wilkinson, James, *Memoirs of My Own Times*. Philadelphia: Abraham Small, 1816.

List of Figures

1. "Progress of the British Army from the Landing in Elk River to the Taking Possession of Philadelphia," 1777, p. vi.

2. "Battle of Paoli," 1782, p. 4.

3. Anthony Wayne, 1796, p. 5.

4. Detail, "Battle of Paoli," p. 6.

5. Johann Ewald, p. 8.

6. William Howe, 1780, p. 12.

7. "Battle of German Town, the 4th October 1777," 1777, p. 14.

8. William Allen, 1746, p. 16.

9. Cliveden, 19th century drawing, p. 17.

10. Lord Cornwallis, 1786, p. 19.

11. Detail, "Battle of Paoli," p. 20.

12. John André, ca. 1780, p. 22.

13. Thomas Musgrave, 1786, p. 24.

14. George Washington, 1787–90, p. 28.

15. John Sullivan, 1776, p. 32.

16. Nathanael Greene, 1784, p. 35.

17. John Eager Howard, 1782, p. 42.

18. "Gin, Engine for drawing the Fuzes out of the Shell, Box with grapeshot, Section of a Petard," 1779, p. 46.

19. Facsimile of William Harris's Signature, p. 49.

20a. American Rifleman & Pennsylvania Infantryman, 1784, p. 51.

20b. Commander-in-Chief's Guard & a Continental Soldier, 1784, p. 52.

21. William Alexander, Lord Stirling, ca. 1858, p. 54.

22. Timothy Pickering, ca. 1792, p. 57.

23. Alexander Hamilton, ca. 1791, p. 60.

24. Henry Knox, 1782, p. 61.

25. "Chew's House," 19th century drawing, p. 62.

26. "Battle of Germantown," 1780, p. 63.

27. "Battle of Germantown," ca. 1790, p. 66.

28. "The Battle of Germantown," 1875, p. 68.

29. "Cliveden Entrance Hall During the Battle of Germantown," ca. 1875, p. 69.

30. Cliveden "Battle Doors," late 19th century, p. 70.

31. Elias Dayton, 1795–1800, p. 71.

32. Thomas Antoine du Plessis-Mauduit, ca. 1900, p. 73.

33. "Battle of Germantown," probably early 19th century, p. 80.

34. Battle of Germantown medal, 19th century, p. 89.

35. Battle of Germantown medal, 19th century, p. 91.

Acknowledgments

There are many individuals who contributed their time and talents to make this book possible. The repositories of historical information are also to be credited, for without their care much of this information would be lost or inaccessible. In addition, grants from the Pew Charitable Trust, the Pennsylvania Historical and Museum Commission, and the Pennsylvania Society of the Sons of the Revolution underwrote research, design and computer costs.

I wish to thank the following organizations and their staffs for their gracious assistance: the David Library of the American Revolution, the Horace Willcox Library at Valley Forge National Historical Park, the collection at Morristown National Historical Park, the Cliveden Collection, the Huntington Library, the Historical Society of Pennsylvania, the Valley Forge Historical Society, the Chester County Historical Society Library and Independence National Historical Park.

Special thanks go to Lee Boyle of the Valley Forge Park Library for his kind assistance and encouragement; Larry Bradbury for his help with information on British officers; Donald Cresswell of the Philadelphia Print Shop for Library of Congress pictorial resources; Karie Diethorn, chief curator of Independence National Historical Park; Jim Kochan, former curator of Morristown National Historical Park, for a bounty of information on the 40th Regiment and numerous unpublished papers, including Hessian papers and the 64th Regiment Light Infantry Company Orderly Book; Paul

Sanborn, who proofread the manuscript and offered help-ful advice; and Larry Schmidt, who provided advice and expertise in New Jersey troop information.

John T. Chew, Jr., a direct descendant of Benjamin Chew, did the photographic copy work.

Deep appreciation goes to Jennifer Esler, Executive Director of Cliveden, who initiated this project in 1988 and has seen the dream of publication become a reality. Jenny's enthusiasm for this work provided much inspira-tion. Thanks also to the Cliveden staff: Anne Roller who helped with editing and computer work; Jean Mitchell who always paid the bills; Elizabeth Laurent who assisted with the illustrations; and Nancy Richards who graciously shared her massive research in the Chew papers. Special hearty huzzahs to Sandy Lloyd for her tireless efforts to organize, edit, illustrate and rework the manuscript: *"O laborum dulce lenimen; redolet lucernam."*

Thomas J. McGuire
Cliveden, July, 1994

Photo Credits

Figures 1 and 7, reproduced by permission of The Huntington Library, San Marino, California; Figures 2, 4, 11 and 26, courtesy of the Valley Forge Historical Society; Figures 3, 8, 14, 16, 17, 21, 22, 23, 31 and 32, courtesy, Independence National Historical Park; Figures 5, 9, 13, 25, 27, 28, 29, 30, 33, 34 and 35, Cliveden Collection. Figures 6, 10, 12, 15, 18, 20 and 24 are in the collection of the Library of Congress and in the public domain.

Colophon

This book was typeset electronically in Adobe Caslon using QuarkXPress. To give a period feeling, the design utilizes many typographic styles and abbreviations that are contemporary with the period during which the Battle of Germantown took place. The maps were created in Aldus FreeHand, using graphic elements and typography from period maps. While an attempt has been made to be faithful to contemporary styles, this book is very much a modern, electronic book, and artistic license has been used to retain readability and to be appealing to twentieth century readers.

✤ ✤ ✤ ✤ ✤ ✤ ✤ ✤ ✤ ✤ ✤ ✤ ✤

List of Maps

MAP 1. *The Position of British Outposts near Cliveden* 27

MAP 2. *Opening Positions 5:30 A.M. yᵉ 4ᵗʰ„ Octʳ„* 38

MAP 3. *The Fight at Mount Pleasant*
5:45 A.M.–6:15 A.M. 43

MAP 4. *The British Flee from MOUNT PLEASANT*
6:15 A.M.–6:30 A.M. 45

MAP 5. *The 40ᵗʰ„ Covers the Retreat of the 2ᵈ„ Batt„*
of Light Infantry and Occupies Cliveden 6:15 A.M. 48

MAP 6. *1ˢᵗ„ Maneuvers around Cliveden*
6:30 A.M.–6:45 A.M. 50

MAP 7. *Wayne & Sullivan Bypass Cliveden 6:45 A.M.* 56

MAP 8. *Action Around Cliveden 7 A.M.* 58

MAP 9. *Action around the House 7:00–8:00 A.M.* 78